Success in Literacy Reading Tests

UNDERSTANDING
YEAR 4
COMPREHENSION
Excellent for all Students, Teachers, Coaches and Parents

Authors

Alan Horsfield   M.Ed, B.A., B. Ed., Dip. Sch. Admin., TESOL, Teaching Cert.
Alan Horsfield has more than 35 years teaching experience in state and private schools in New South Wales and International Schools in Papua New Guinea. He was employed by UNSW (EAA) as an English Research Officer involved in the construction of school tests for English and Mathematics. Alan is a published writer of children's fiction, educational material and school texts.

Elaine Horsfield   M.A. (Theatre Studies), B.A. (Theatre Media), Teaching Cert.
Elaine Horsfield has more than 25 years teaching experience in Primary Schools both with the New South Wales Department of Education and in International Schools in Papua New Guinea. She worked with secondary students as coordinator of the NSW Talent Development Project. Elaine is a published writer of children's poetry and educational books.

Editor:
Warwick Marlin B.Sc. Dip.Ed.

Publisher:
Five Senses Education
ABN: 16 001 414437
2/195 Prospect Highway
Seven Hills NSW Australia 2147
sevenhills@fivesenseseducation.com.au
www.fivesenseseducation.com.au

Trade Enquiries:
Phone (02) 9838 9265
Fax (02) 9838 8982
Email: fsonline@fivesenseseducation.com.au

Understanding Year 4 Comprehension
ISBN: 978-1-76032-018-8
1ˢᵗ Edition: May 2014
Copyright: Alan Horsfield © Five Senses Education Pty. Ltd. © Warwick Marlin

AUTHOR'S ACKNOWLEDGEMENTS

Warwick Marlin, my editor, whose advice and guidance have been very much appreciated.

Roger Furniss, at Five Senses Education for publishing my books.

And above all, to **Jones**, my typesetter, for a high standard of typesetting, layout and artwork. A very special thank you for your time, patience, attention to detail, and overall quality of your work.

PARENTS

This book tells you what the teacher often does not have the time to explain in detail – the intricacies of a wide variation in text types and the testing strategies used by Australian testing institutions to asses progress in Literacy. It will give you confidence to support your children by reinforcing what is being taught in schools and what is being tested, especially Reading Comprehension.

TEACHERS

This book introduces text types and test question types Australian students should understand to maximise internal and external Reading Tests. Reading tests may involve comprehension as well as related grammar questions. It eliminates the need to wade through lengthy curriculum documents and it provides a clear and easy to follow format for teachers to use. Teachers can also confidently recommend this book to parents as it supports classroom activities and exercises.

B. Ed., Dip Ed. PRIMARY SCHOOL TEACHERS

This book contains a variety of recognised primary school text types with question sets that will improve reading comprehension and improved results in reading tests. It acts as a quick reference book for teachers in the early years of teaching, when there is so much to learn.

AVAILABILITY OF MATHEMATICS BOOKS

All of the Mathematics books below have been produced by the same editor and publisher, and in many cases the same author (Warwick Marlin). Therefore they all incorporate the same high presentation and philosophy. They can be purchased directly from Five Senses Education, but they are also available in most educational bookshops throughout NSW and Australia (and also some selected bookshops in New Zealand).

New National Curriculum titles

The eight school titles listed directly below have been rewritten and updated in recent years to closely follow the New National Curriculum. **'All levels'** means that the books have been written for students of most ability groups (weak, average and gifted). The graded tests at the end of each chapter ensure that students of most ability groups are extended to their full potential.

❏	YEAR 1	ALL LEVELS
❏	YEAR 2	ALL LEVELS
❏	YEAR 3	ALL LEVELS
❏	YEAR 4	ALL LEVELS
❏	YEAR 5	ALL LEVELS
❏	YEAR 6	ALL LEVELS
❏	YEAR 7	ALL LEVELS
❏	YEAR 8	ALL LEVELS

Other titles in this series

The titles listed below are also available, but they will be fully updated during 2014 and 2015 to also closely follow the new curriculum. However, in the meantime, please note, that these books still adequately address the main features of the new syllabus. We firmly believe that the major topics explained in these titles, and our user friendly presentation and development of the different topics, will always continue to form the vital foundations for all future study and applications of mathematics. This is especially so for the titles up to, and including Year 10 Advanced.

❏	YEAR 9 & 10	INTERMEDIATE
❏	YEAR 9 & 10	ADVANCED
❏	YEAR 11 & 12	GENERAL MATHS
❏	YEAR 11	EXTENSION 1
❏	YEAR 12	EXTENSION 1

Also by the same Author and Editor (Warwick Marlin)

❏	ESSENTIAL EXERCISES YEAR 1	ALL LEVELS
❏	ESSENTIAL EXERCISES YEAR 2	ALL LEVELS
❏	ESSENTIAL EXERCISES YEAR 3	ALL LEVELS
❏	ESSENTIAL EXERCISES YEAR 4	ALL LEVELS
❏	ESSENTIAL EXERCISES YEAR 5	ALL LEVELS
❏	ESSENTIAL EXERCISES YEAR 6	ALL LEVELS

Developed & written in 2012, this excellent new series of books closely follows the Australian National Curriculum.

CONTENTS

Year 4 Comprehension Passages and Exercises

"So it is with children who learn to read fluently and well. They begin to take flight into whole new worlds as effortlessly as young birds take to the sky."

William James

Understanding Year 4 Comprehension
A. Horsfield © Five Senses Education © W. Marlin

UNDERSTANDING YEAR 4 ENGLISH TESTING

This is an important year in the child's education. Groundwork commenced in the earlier years leads to a more formal development of literacy understanding in Year 4. It is a time when the school and the home continue to work closely together. It is important that the home has a positive attitude to school and education, and also provides support with an abundance of practical activities in an environment that stimulates curiosity and enjoyment in reading and writing. The more literacy experiences the child has, the more realistic and practical will be the child's foundation in literacy in later years, and the more confidence the child will have.

It is in these early years the child continues to move from literal comprehension of text to the more abstract. What is implied becomes more and more important. This transition will vary from child to child. At times, we all read different 'messages' from the text. It is also important to understand that we don't necessarily grasp the intended meaning on a first reading. Re-reading is an important strategy.

Remember: Do not have unreal expectations of what your child can read. Don't 'push' too hard, especially with the more formal written work. Keep literacy fun, especially in reading, and then attitudes will be positive. At times it is fun to read something that is not so challenging!

The best way to succeed in any test is to practice.
An old Chinese proverb sums it up well:

I enjoy a little bit of recreational reading every day!

> I hear, I forget;
> I see, I remember;
> I do, I understand.

The NAPLAN testing program for Australian Schools treats three strands of English. **Reading tests,** which include the comprehension of a variety of text types, **Writing tests,** which focus on writing a narrative, a persuasive text or a recount, **Language Convention tests**, which include Spelling, Punctuation and Grammar.

All three strands are interrelated in the 'real world'. As the National Curriculum states, "Teaching and learning programs should balance and integrate all three strands' (see: http://www.australian curriculum.edu.au/Year4).

This book is based on Year levels not Stages. (There are three basic primary school stages. Year 3 and Year 4 make up Stage 2.) In Year 4 there is a strong emphasis on comprehending a variety of text types. Not all text types get the same attention. The study of persuasive text is more complex and subtle than, say, following directions. As families and society are a complex mix of differing experiences, children will have different exposure to different text types. Individual children will develop different strengths and weaknesses.

This book focuses specifically on Reading but the skills learned in Reading can assist in the development of the child's Writing skills. The skills learned in the Language Convention strand can improve both Reading and Writing.

That is why we have included a Literacy Tip (**Lit Tip**) component at the end of each set of questions. These may help with any Language Convention questions that come up in standardised reading tests as well as adding 'tricks' that may improve the quality of Writing test responses.

HOW TO USE THIS BOOK EFFECTIVELY

As stated, this book's primary aim is to improve Reading comprehension with some input into Language Convention. Obviously the Speaking, Listening and Handwriting strands are not included.

The passages are not selected in any specific order but are intended to present a wide variation of text types. Those most likely to be part of the testing situation are treated more often. The text type is shown at the top of each passage as well as in the **Year 4 Comprehension Passages and Exercises** chart that follows.

There will be differences of focus from school to school, as teachers tend to select topics in varying sequences according to their program at a particular time in a year. Some students maybe involved in accelerated promotion, enrichment or remedial activities.

ABOUT THE EXERCISES

The intent of the 40 passages is to provide one passage per week for each school week. This should not impinge too much on obligations set by the school/class teacher for homework and research. There is one easier **practice passage** provided to make the child aware of a range of question types that maybe encountered.

Children need not work through the exercises from 1 to 40 in the order in which they are presented in this book. There is the option of practicing a particular text type, e.g. poetry.

The Comprehension Answers and the Lit Tip Answers are on separate pages at the back of the book.

Reading texts can be based on either **Factual** or **Literary** texts.
Year 4 question types often include the skills of:

- **Locating** such things as information, a sequence of events, literary techniques, grammar convention and vocabulary features,

- **Identifying** genres, the purpose of a text, literary techniques, appropriate punctuation, word meanings,

- **Interpreting** visual information, multiple pieces of information, language style,

- **Inferring** next event in a text, reason for a character's action, outcomes, the effect of tense and person, and

- **Synthesising** the tone of a text, the main idea in a text, a character's motivation, the writer's opinion, the intended audience for a text.

These above skills are more or less arranged in an order of difficulty.

Allan Horsfield   M.Ed., B.A., B. Ed., Dip. Sch. Admin., TESOL, Teaching Cert.
Elaine Horsfield   M. A. (Theatre Studies), B. A. (Theatre Media), Teaching Cert.

Understanding Year 4 Comprehension
A. Horsfield © Five Senses Education © W. Marlin

TEST SOURCES

The questions, information and practice provided by this book will benefit the student sitting for the following tests.

Externally produced tests

NAPLAN (National Assessment – Literacy and Numeracy) Used Australia wide.
PAT (-R) (Progressive Achievements Tests – Reading)
ICAS (International Competitions and Assessments for Schools) Run by EAA.
Selective Schools and High Schools Placement Tests (Most states have tests specific to that state's educational policy.)
Scholarship Tests
ACER (Australian Council for Educational Research) Scholarship tests (Most states have tests specific to that state's educational policy)
AusVELS (Australian Curriculum in Victoria Essential Learning Standards)
Independent Assessment Agencies (e. g. Academic Assessment Services)
ISA (International Schools Assessment) run by ACER

There may be a number of other independent, external sources for literacy testing.

School produced tests

- year tests
- class tests
- school tests

Information provided in this book may also be beneficial in certain competitions run by commercial enterprises.

A number of commercial publishers also provide books of practice tests.

The purpose of testing

Testing has a variety of purposes and the purpose will often determine the type of test administered. Tests may be used to:
- determine what the student has learned
- rank students in order of ability
- select the most worthy students for a school or class
- determine the strength and weakness of classroom teaching
- determine any 'short-comings' in a school's educational program
- ascertain the effectiveness of certain teaching strategies
- evaluate the effectiveness of departmental/official syllabuses

A BRIEF SUMMARY OF SOME QUESTION FORMATS

Look at the nursery rhyme, Jack and Jill, as the text for a set of questions.

1 Jack and Jill went up the hill To <u>fetch</u> a pail of water. Jack fell down and broke his crown And Jill came tumbling after.	2 Up Jack got and home he trot As fast as he could caper, And went to bed to __(4)__ his head With vinegar and brown paper.

Many tests are based on multiple-choice responses. You are given a choice of four (sometimes three) possible answers (options) to choose from.
Some will take the form of a question: You may have to circle a letter or shade a box.

1. Why did Jack go up the hill?
- A   to meet Jill
- B   to get a pail of water
- C   to have a sleep
- D   to collect paper

The question could have been framed so that you have to complete a sentence.

2. Jack went up the hill to
- A   meet Jill
- B   get a pail of water
- C   have a sleep
- D   collect paper

Some questions may have to do with word or phrase meanings.

3. Choose the word that could best replace *fetch* as used in the text.
- A   fill   B   find   C   get   D   empty

(Did you notice the different lay-out of the options? They were across the page.)

4. Which word would best go in the space labelled (4) in stanza 2?
- A   mend   B   wash   C   find   D   scratch

Sometimes you might have to work out the sequence in which events occured.

5. Write the numbers 1 to 4 in the boxes to show the correct order in which events occured in the rhyme. The first one has been done for you.

1	Jack went up the hill.
	Jack went to bed.
	Jill fell down the hill.
	Jack hurried home.

Some questions are called free response questions. You will have to write an answer.

6. How many people went up the hill? Write your answer on the line? _____

Sometimes you might have to decide if something is TRUE or FALSE.

7. Tick the box to show if this statement is TRUE or FALSE.

Jack went up the hill to get brown paper. TRUE ☐   FALSE ☐

There will be times when you will have to read the whole text and make a judgment.

8. You know that Jack was seriously injured because he
- A   rushed home
- B   had cracked his skull
- C   didn't wait for Jill
- D   left his pail of water behind

9. Sometimes you might have to decide if, according to the text, a statement is FACT or OPINION.

Answers: 1. B, 2. B, 3. C, 4. A, 5. (1, 4, 2, 3), 6. 2, 7. FALSE, 8. B

Understanding Year 4 Comprehension
A. Horsfield © Five Senses Education © W. Marlin

Read the recount *The Mystery of the Two Chimneys.*

The Mystery of the Two Chimneys

While on a family holiday we drove through a State Forest near Lake Tinaroo. Imagine our surprise to suddenly come across two chimneys in a small clearing. Dad stopped the station wagon and we got out.
We discovered a plaque near the chimneys.
It stated the area was once a soldier settlement - land given to soldiers returning from World War 1 (1914 - 18). In 1924 Bill Hanley and Thomas Clark built a house on the site and ran a sawmill nearby until 1955 when the Tinaroo Dam was constructed.

These pictures from the plaque, tell a story.

1

The original soldier settlement house.
The original settler abandoned his house and left the area.

2

The original Hanley and Clark mill before it was moved to the village of Kairi.

3

This Kauri pine <u>butt</u> log contained enough timber for several houses.

4

Logging machinery - 1925 style.
On one day this tractor hauled two giant logs from the one tree to the mill.

5

The house built on the returned soldiers' site by Bill Hanley and Thomas Clark. It featured the two chimneys.

Remember: The person telling the story in the text is called the **narrator**. The narrator uses such terms as *I* and *we*. It is the **author** who actually writes the text. It seems to be a different person.

Understanding Recounts

Circle a letter or write an answer for questions 1 to 8.

1. How did the narrator's family arrive at the site of the two chimneys?

    A   They crossed Lake Tinaroo.
    B   They came on a tractor hauling two giant logs.
    C   They arrived in a station wagon.
    D   They walked in through a State Forest.

2. Who was with the narrator when she looked at the two chimneys?

    A   her family   B   a returned soldier
    C   a timber cutter   D   Bill Hanley and Thomas Clark

3. The two chimneys were once part of

    A   the original saw mill   B   a returned soldier's homestead
    C   a timber hauler's home   D   the Hanley and Clark house

4. Write the numbers 1 to 4 in the boxes to show the correct order in which events occured in the recount. The first one (1) has been done for you.

☐	a sawmill was established near the site
☐	the narrator's family arrived at the site in a station wagon
☐	the Hanley and Clark home fell into disrepair
1	a returned soldier built a home at the site

5. When did the Bill Hanley and Thomas Clark's sawmill stop operating?

Write your answer on the line? _____

6. Tick the box to show if this statement is TRUE or FALSE. The mystery of the two chimneys was solved for the family.

TRUE ☐   FALSE ☐

7. What part of a tree is its *butt?*

    A   the whole trunk   B   the underground roots
    C   the lower part of the trunk   D   the discarded parts of the tree

8. How would you best describe the Bill Hanley and Thomas Clark house compared to the returned soldier's house?

The Bill Hanley and Thomas Clark house was

    A   much the same as the soldier's house
    B   more lavish than the soldier's house
    C   lacking the style of the soldier's house
    D   less suitable for the area than the soldier's house

Answers: 1. C   2. A   3. D   4. (3, 4, 2, 1)   5. 1955   6. TRUE   7. C   8. B

Understanding Year 4 Comprehension
A. Horsfield © Five Senses Education © W. Marlin

Year 4 Comprehension Passages and Exercises

Each of the 40 passages has a set of eight comprehension and language questions, based upon that text. Following the questions is a section called **Lit Tip** (short for Literacy Tips). These are gems of information that are intended to develop the child's responses to Language Conventions questions arising in texts and tests. They may also be beneficial when answering questions in Language Convention (Grammar) papers or when completing Writing assessment tasks.

Understanding Year 4 Comprehension
A. Horsfield © Five Senses Education © W. Marlin

The Carousel

The old man shut the gate with a clang, then roared to his assistant, "Let her go!"

With a creak and a groan of old gears the carousel began to move and then the organ music began.

Olivia patted her horse's mane. As the horse began to move up and down she settled herself more comfortably into the saddle. The ride was taking her around to the other side, away from the food stalls and amusement tents.

It was then she heard the crash. Metal garbage bins rattling into the gutter – followed by yells of anger from Perrin St. Olivia twisted in her saddle but all she could see was the old grandstand nearby sailing past. Then it was the fence to the town oval.

"Hooligans," muttered the old man as he worked his way through the bobbing horsesand around the revolving platform.

As the carousel continued its circuit Olivia could saw that he was right. There were garbage bins on their side in front of Mr O'Hare's barbershop. She could also see two boys racing across the grass of the fair grounds. One was that horrible Jimmy Dean!

Mr O'Hare was in hot pursuit of the boys gaining on the slower boys.

Olivia suddenly recognised the younger boy. It was Reece, her brother! He wouldn't have pushed over the bins. She just knew it. He was just too shy. But it looked as if he could be the one paying for it.

Keep going Olivia silently begged. Her horse was almost level with Reece and he was tiring. There was anguish in his tear-stained face.

At that moment Reece recognised Olivia.

Without thinking Olivia jumped from her horse, leant over the side of the carousel and with outstretched arms grabbed Reece and swung him up to safety.

Understanding Narratives   Circle a letter or write an answer for questions 1 to 8.

1. Who was riding on the carousel?
    A   Reece   B   Olivia
    C   Mr O'Hare   D   Jimmy Dean

2. What was the first sound Olivia heard after the old man roared, "Let her go!"
    A   garbage bins rolling about   B   organ music
    C   Mr O'Hare shouting   D   the groan of the carousel's gears

3. The text states that there was *anguish* on Reece's face. This means he was feeling
    A   excited   B   reckless
    C   distressed   D   angry

4. Olivia felt certain that Reece had not upturned the garbage bins because he was
    A   no where near the barber's shop   B   too shy to do something like that
    C   waiting to get on the carousel   D   running away from hooligans

5. Choose the word that best describes how Olivia felt when she got on her horse?
    A   frightened   B   relaxed
    C   unsure   D   confused

6. According to the text, which statement is correct?
    A   Jimmy Dean tried to climb on the carousel.
    B   The carousel assistant checked the horses as the carousel revolved.
    C   The carousel horses were able to move up and down.
    D   Olivia knew immediately what had made the old man angry.

7. What could Olivia see when she heard the garbage bins rolling on the footpath?
    Write your answer on this line._____

8. What part of speech is the word *safety* as used in the text?
    A   noun   B   verb   C   adjective   D   preposition

Need to try another narrative passage? Check the contents page.

Lit Tip 1 – Improve your literacy skills   Direct and indirect speech

Words spoken can be recorded as direct speech or indirect speech.

Direct speech uses the actual words spoken in inverted commas (quotation marks).
An example: "Hooligans", muttered the old man.
This could have been written: The old man muttered, "Hooligans."

Indirect speech reports the meaning of what has been said, but not the exact words.
An example: The doctor said <u>that</u> the cut on my arm was not serious.
Indirect speech often uses the word <u>that</u> to introduce the reported words.

Look at these three sentences. Tick those that are written using indirect speech.

1. Jack asked the plumber if he could fix the hose. ☐

2. "Can you fix the hose?" Jack asked the plumber. ☐

3. Mum said that it was time for bed. ☐

Understanding Year 4 Comprehension
A. Horsfield © Five Senses Education © W. Marlin

Animals' Houses

Of animals' houses
Two sorts are found-
Those which are square ones
And those which are round.

Square is a hen house,
A kennel, a sty;
Cows have square houses
And so have I.

A snail's shell is curly,
A bird's nest is round;
Rabbits have twisty burrows
Underground.

But the fish in the bowl
And the fish at sea-
Their houses are round
As a house can be.

James Reeves (1909 – 1978)

Understanding Poetry   Circle a letter or write an answer for questions 1 to 8.

1. Which animal lives in a curly house?
    - A   rabbit
    - B   snail
    - C   goldfish
    - D   bird

2. A sty is a house for a
    - A   dog   B   hen   C   cow   D   pig

3. Where do rabbits have their homes?
    - A   under the ground
    - B   in a nest
    - C   near a garden
    - D   by a vegetable patch

4. What word from the poem rhymes with *sty*?
    - A   curly   B   sea   C   I   D   house

5. Tick a box for TRUE or FALSE for this statement.
    The poet doesn't have his own house

    TRUE   ☐   FALSE   ☐

6. According to the poem which creature has the roundest house?
    - A   the cow
    - B   the rabbit
    - C   the hen
    - D   the fish

7. On the line write the name of a house for a dog._____

8. How many different sorts of houses does the poet describe?
    - A   two   B   three   C   five   D   nine

Need to try another poem? Check the contents page.

Lit Tip 2 – Improve your literacy skills   Understanding rhyme

Most words that rhyme end with the same arrangement of letters.

For example: c<u>at</u>, r<u>at</u>, th<u>at</u>;   re<u>ach</u>, p<u>each</u>;   tr<u>easure</u>, pl<u>easure</u>

Sometimes rhyming words may look different, e.g. write/flight;   answer/dancer

Sometimes words that look different can rhyme, e.g. blue/grew;   bough/cow

Circle the word that does *not* rhyme with the other words in each line.

1.	dead	bread	said	Fred	bead
2.	some	dumb	hum	drum	home

Circle the word that rhymes with mother.

3.	father	uncle	brother	mower	rather

Circle the word that rhymes with were.

4.	there	fur	where	here	share

Understanding Year 4 Comprehension
A. Horsfield © Five Senses Education © W. Marlin

Read the persuasive text *People Should Drink Green Tea.*

People Should Drink Green Tea

People, usually adults, who drink green tea seem to think it's the best thing since, well… since sliced bread. Why is this so? This flavourful beverage offers many health benefits for regular tea drinkers.

Firstly green tea is a superb fat fighter. It contains an ingredient, that helps burn body fat especially belly fat. It can help with weight loss.

Secondly it keeps energy stable by balancing sugar levels in the blood. Changes in blood sugar level can cause fatigue, irritability, and the desire for unhealthy foods.

Thirdly scientists think it may be helpful in the fight against several types of cancer, including lung cancer.

Another reason to switch to green tea is because it may prevent skin damage and wrinkling and other signs of aging. It may also reduce the risk of arthritis (aches in bone joints) in people as they age.

But, if you want a really good reason – it tastes great. You might not be a tea (or coffee) drinker but now's the time to get your parents to make the change. Give them the reasons and tell them green tea contains a lot less caffeine than coffee or black tea. Buy them green teabags at the supermarket and make your mum and dad a surprise cup of tea one day for morning tea.

Mmmmm. Green tea. Really enjoyable.

Source: http://www.care2.com/greenliving/9-reasons-to-drink-green-tea-daily.html

Understanding Persuasions Circle a letter or write an answer for questions 1 to 8.

1. The writer suggests people should drink green tea because it
   A   is the most popular morning drink   B   has health benefits
   C   goes well with sliced bread   D   is cheaper than coffee

2. Drinking green tea
   A   reduces the risk of arthritis   B   prevents lung cancer
   C   stops skin from wrinkling   D   does all of the previously mentioned

3. Arthritis is a complaint to do with
   A   bone joints   B   skin damage
   C   skin cancer   D   being overweight

4. What can changes in blood sugar levels do to people?
   A   keep them awake   B   increase their appetite
   C   put on belly fat   D   make them irritable

5. When the writer uses *Mmmmm* it indicates that she is
   A   doubtful about the information   B   imagining a great taste
   C   trying to make up her mind   D   getting tired

6. What is meant by the word *ingredient* as it is used in the text?
   A   something that causes heartburn
   B   a special type of diet food
   C   a substance that combines with other substances
   D   food that does not include sugar or fat

7. Name one drink from the text that has more caffeine than green tea.

   Write your answer on this line._____

8. Who is the writer trying to persuade to buy green tea?
   A   fathers   B   elderly people
   C   mothers   D   the reader

Need to try another persuasion passage? Check the contents page.

Lit Tip 3 – Improve your literacy skills   How to use dashes

A dash (–) is a form of punctuation used to introduce interrupted speech or ideas.
  • Meg replied vaguely, "I – I – told you I can't –"
  • We watched two TV shows last night – I didn't like either one.

It is often used in dates or periods of time.
  • Jack Brown (1973–2011) This shows the years of Jack Brown's life.

If the person has not yet died you can still use a dash, e.g. Mary Brown (1974 –)

Read the text " people should drink green tea" again and highlight the two words separated by a dash.

Here are some dates for people's lives. Circle the person's name who is still alive.

  Ann Green (1852–1896)   Raj Nambun (1956–2013)   Pete Gray (1978–)

Remember: a dash is **not** a hyphen.

Understanding Year 4 Comprehension
A. Horsfield © Five Senses Education © W. Marlin

Read the procedure *How to Eat an Ice Cream.*

How to Eat an Ice Cream

Everyone loves ice cream, especially in a cone. Trouble with cones is the ice cream can start melting before you finish eating it. Sometimes it can make your brain numb because the ice cream is cold. So, what do you do?

Firstly, buy an ice cream at an ice cream <u>parlour</u> that sells ice creams in cones. Have an adult to help you do this.

Don't waste any ice cream. As soon as you have made your purchase quickly lick any ice cream that may be melting over the edge of the cone.

Wrap a paper serviette around the base of the cone.
Ice cream parlours usually provide one. The serviette will help prevent the ice cream from melting – and stop your hands from getting cold – and sticky.

Find a safe place nearby to sit and enjoy your ice cream in peace. This means you won't get bumped by someone and your ice cream ends up on your clothes – or the footpath!

Lick the ice cream around the top of the cone. Watch for dribbles over the side. It's best not to take bites of ice cream. The cold will make your teeth ache. If you take bites make sure they are small bites.

Eat the cone from the top once the ice cream is finished. Don't bite the base of the cone. There may be melted ice cream in the base that could drip out and make your hands sticky.

Once you have finished eating wipe your face, and hands if necessary, with a serviette then put it _____(4)_____.

Understanding Procedures   Circle a letter or write an answer for questions 1 to 8.

1. According to the text the first thing you must do if you want to eat an ice cream is to
    A   get a paper serviette
    B   look for a suitable place to sit
    C   buy an ice cream at an ice cream shop
    D   keep your ice cream cold

2. Once you have an ice cream you should
    A   leave the ice cream shop
    B   avoid being bumped by other people
    C   lick off any melting ice cream
    D   keep your ice cream cold

3. A suitable synonym (a word with a similar meaning) for *parlour* would be
    A   pantry   B   store room   C   counter   D   shop

4. The final words have been left out at (4) in the text.
    The most suitable conclusion for text at (4) would be
    A   in a garbage bin   B   near a drain
    C   in your pocket   D   on the footpath

5. The writer suggests you shouldn't bite into your ice cream because
    A   you will finish your ice cream too quickly
    B   it will make your teeth ache
    C   it causes your ice cream to melt
    D   makes your brain feel numb

6. According to the text you shouldn't bite the bottom off the cone because
    A   melted ice cream could get on your hands
    B   the serviette will get sticky
    C   it's the coldest part of the ice cream cone
    D   it's not allowed in an ice cream parlour

7. What word from the text means to *a thin stream of small drops*?
    Write your answer on this line._____

8. According to the text, you are unlikely to drop your ice cream if you
    A   wrap it in a serviette   B   eat it as quickly as possible
    C   lick around the top of the cone   D   find a safe place to sit

Need to try another procedure passage? Check the contents page.

Lit Tip 4 – Improve your literacy skills   Synonyms and antonyms

Synonyms are words with similar meanings: fast - quick, arid - dry, old - elderly

Antonyms are words with opposite meanings: fast - slow, arid - wet, beginning - end

1. Give a synonym then an antonym for begin. _____, _____

2. Circle the synonyms for sleepy.
    yawn   tired   bed   drowsy   napping

3. Circle the antonym for cold.
    bold   heater   shiver   sweat   hot

Understanding Year 4 Comprehension
A. Horsfield © Five Senses Education © W. Marlin

5 Read the recount *Postcard from Fiji.*

Postcard from Fiji

Here is the front and the back of a postcard sent from Fiji.

Front

The ride of a lifetime

The Coral Coast Train

Back

Hi Elle,
How are you?
I'm having a great time. After
breakfast today I had a swim
in the Hilux Hotel pool. The weather
is *awesome* over here. After my
swim Mum took the family down
to a cute little station. We went
for a train ride. The engine was
an old cane train steam engine.
We crossed a river, then went
though some sugarcane fields, past
a Fijian village and ended up at a
cafe by a long sandy beach. I had
another swim. Wish you were here!
Say hello to Reanna and Jo for me.
Lucie S   xx

To
Elle Hana

2 Flower Lane

Pacific Port

Queensland

Australia

Affix
stamp
here

Coral Coast train Nadi, Fiji

Understanding Recounts   Circle a letter or write an answer for questions 1 to 8.

1. Who wrote the postcard?
   A   Elle   B   Lucie   C   Jo   D   Reanna

2. As used in the text, which word could be used instead of *awesome*?
   A   friendly   B   frightening
   C   marvellous   D   changeable

3. The box in the top right hand corner of the back of the card reads: _Affix_ stamp here.
   What is the best meaning for *affix* as it is used on the postcard?
   A   stick   B   attach   C   fasten   D   add

4. Where did Lucie have her first swim?
   A   in a river near the train line   B   at a Fijian beach
   C   in the Hilux Hotel pool   D   near a cafe after a train trip

5. What does Lucie really enjoy doing on her holiday?
   A   having breakfast   B   going for train rides
   C   visiting railway stations D   having a swim

6. Who was with Lucie on her Fijian holiday?
   A   Jo   B   Reanna   C   her family   D   Elle Hana

7. Which word best describes how the postcard writer was enjoying the holiday?
   The writer was
   A   satisfied   B   thrilled   C   disappointed   D   surprised

8. Write the numbers 1 to 4 in the boxes to show the correct order in which events occur.
   The first one (1) has been done for you.

	the family go to the station
1	the writer has a swim in the Hilux Hotel pool
	the train arrives at a place where there is a cafe
	the train passes by sugarcane fields

Need to try another recount passage? Check the contents page.

Lit Tip 5 – Improve your literacy skills   **Compound words**

Compound words are two or more words joined to make a new word.

Examples: daylight, outside, whenever, basketball, nevertheless

Take care with prefixes: Prefixes are small groups of letters that can change the meaning of a word, e.g. underline, replace, display.

Circle the word in each line that is a compound word.

1. substation   highway   insult   misfit   careful

2. bookmark   rattle   dessert   mountain   uniform

Circle the word in this line that is not a compound word.

3. saucepan   sandstone   television   towbar   highlight

Understanding Year 4 Comprehension
A. Horsfield © Five Senses Education © W. Marlin

Battery Drain

Low battery is a frustrating occurrence for many people using electronic communication equipment. Many newer devices have a battery with a ten-hour use before recharging becomes necessary. Ten hours is about the limit you can expect before the loss of features. All devices use Lithium-ion battery technology, which allows users to recharge their devices before they have been completely drained. There are 'tricks' for maximising the life of a battery.

Email

Stop your device from collecting emails automatically. You can program your device to fetch emails from the server less frequently or only when you manually check your email.

Notifications

Your devices have features that includes all sorts of alerts. Leaving them on uses battery power because the device is constantly checking with the server to find any alerts directed to your device. Turn off those you don't need.

Updates

Software designers who write codes for the operating systems (OS) are involved in making the system more efficient regarding its power use. Owners should always keep their OS up to date
to ensure they are getting maximum benefits from their device.

GPS (Global Positioning System)

Many apps incorporate a GPS system, even down to finding the closest ATM. Turn it off until it is required.

Understanding Explanations   Circle a letter for questions 1 to 8.

1. The word *battery drain* as used in the title refers to
   A   disposing of batteries   B   misuse of old batteries
   C   batteries losing power   D   recycling batteries

2. Alerts can be responsible for the loss of battery power because
   A   the device uses power when constantly checking for alerts
   B   too many alerts are sent to your server
   C   devices search for alerts even when the device is switched off
   D   most alerts are heavy users of battery power

3. The initials OS stands for
   A   old stock   B   operating system
   C   owner's server   D   over supply

4. The word *tricks* as used in the text means a
   A   mischievous practical jokes   B   schemes meant to deceive
   C   pleasant surprises   D   clever ways of doing something

5. The text suggests that to be more efficient when using emails it is best to
   A   program the device to check for emails at set intervals
   B   switch the device off when not checking emails
   C   not to respond to emails unless you have to
   D   collect emails before sending emails

6. According to the text which statement is CORRECT?
   A   Never use your device to find an ATM.
   B   Battery life is limited to ten hours for all apps.
   C   Update software when it becomes available.
   D   It's important to keep the GPS function switched on.

7. Which word from the text means having *the latest and most modern versions*?
   A   features   B   users   C   benefits   D   updates

8. According to the text the advantages of Lithium-ion batteries is that they
   A   are easy to replace   B   can be recharged before fully drained
   C   include 'tricks' for the user   D   are cheaper than other batteries

Need to try another explanation passage? Check the contents page

---

Lit Tip 6 – Improve your literacy skills   **Using initials**

Often places and organisations are referred to by their initials. E.g. South Australia is called SA. The United Nations is called the UN.

An automatic teller machine is called an ATM. For such names we use capital letters without using full stops. If we post a letter it might go to a Post Office box. We write PO Box. Small words usually don't get capitals or even included. Example DET for the Department of Education and Training

1. What would be the initials for: personal identification number? _____

2. University of New South Wales? _____

3. National Assessment Program - Literacy and Numeracy _____

Some initials do not use capitals: scuba = self-contained underwater breathing apparatus. It has become a word using lower case letters.

Understanding Year 4 Comprehension
A. Horsfield © Five Senses Education © W. Marlin

Gillang Bay

The bus reached the top of the steep climb and paused. It then turned left at the T-intersection onto a narrow road that followed the high crest of the narrow ridge around the horseshoe-shaped bay far below. The road they were following was once the lip of an enormous volcano. The lip had eroded over the centuries so that it now looked like the teeth of a badly maintained bushman's saw.

Brian gazed out of the bus's dusty window. The whole landscape below, now dotted with homes and quiet villages, had once come spewing out of the depths of the earth in great, red lava flows.

As Brian knew, from projects they had done at school, Gillang Bay was the flooded crater of an ancient volcano. After the first eruption the eastern side had been blasted out by a massive volcanic explosion and the sea had gushed in.

Numerous little bays and inlets were formed when the lava flows had hardened. Millions of years later small fishing villages nestled along the peaceful foreshore fields amongst dark green trees and a sprinkling of small grazing fields for cattle.

The bus chugged up a small, steep rise and when it reached the top Brian could see over the headlands guarding the passage into the bay the mighty expanse of the Pacific Ocean. In the distance the horizon and sky merged as if they were part of the same backdrop to the ridge around Gillang Bay.

Understanding Descriptions
Circle a letter, write an answer or tick a box for questions 1 to 8.

1. The text is mainly a description of
   A   a volcanic eruption
   B   a bus trip
   C   the view from a ridge
   D   a country road

2. How did Brian come to know so much about Gillang Bay?
   A   he has learned about it at school
   B   he studied it through the bus window
   C   he lived at Gillang Bay
   D   Gillang Bay was an industrial area

3. Which word best describes the communities around Gillang Bay?
   A   busy   B   hectic   C   polluted   D   peaceful

4. Choose the words from the text that are an example of a simile.
   A   the bus chugged up a small steep rise
   B   like the teeth of a badly maintained bushman's saw
   C   spewing out of the depths of the earth in great, red, lava flows
   D   the bus reached the top of the steep climb and paused

5. What was an important occupation in Gillang Bay
   A   bus driving
   B   cleaning windows
   C   fishing
   D   cattle raising

6. Write a word from the text that indicates the bus was not big and powerful.
   Write your answer on this line._____

7. Which shape best shows the shape of Gillang Bay?
   A   B   C   D

8. Tick TRUE or FALSE
   The homes around Gillang Bay were in danger of being flooded

   TRUE ☐   FALSE ☐

Need to try another description passage? Check the contents page.

Lit Tip 7 – Improve your literacy skills   **Similes**

A **simile** is a way of comparing something to something else to make a description more vivid.

Examples: Jayden was <u>as big as an elephant</u>. We know Jayden was very big.

Lisa eats <u>like a pig</u>. We know that Lisa is a very messy eater.

These cup cakes <u>taste like rotten apples</u>. The cup cakes taste really awful.

Complete these three similes. Try to avoid common sayings.

(Note: Given answers are examples only)

1. The actor was as old as a/an/the _____.

2. Uncle Jim still smokes like a/an _____!

3. The new moon looked like a/an _____.

Understanding Year 4 Comprehension
A. Horsfield © Five Senses Education © W. Marlin

Insects

Insects belong to a group of animals called arthropods. Arthropods have jointed legs and a hard body wall. Some other animals that belong to the arthropod group are prawns, spiders, crabs and lobsters. Insects differ from other arthropods because they have six legs.

The number of insect species is believed to be between six and ten million. That's not the number of insects but the number of different types!

Insects bodies have three parts, the thorax, abdomen and head. Insects have two antennae. Insects have three pairs of legs. Insects are cold blooded. The life cycle of an insect begins with an egg, which then hatches into a larva (or grub).

Bees, termites and ants live in well-organised social colonies.

For protection insects may sting, nip or give off a really bad smell. Many are masters of camouflage.

Some strange insect facts

- Only male crickets chirp.
- Some insects such as water striders, are able to walk on the surface of water.
- Silkworms, in their cocoon stage, are used as the producers of silk. Those that survive become moths as adults.
- Some cicadas can make sounds nearly 120 decibels loud. That can cause ear damage in humans!
- Most insects hatch from eggs. Female mosquitoes drink blood in order to obtain nutrients needed to produce eggs.
- An ant is a <u>typical</u>, very common insect.

Remember: Spiders are not insects. They have eight legs.

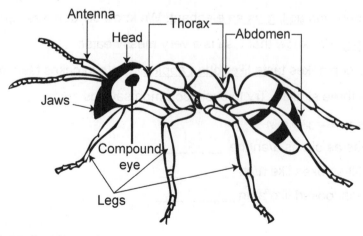

Understanding Reports   Circle a letter or write an answer for questions 1 to 8.

1. This report is mainly a text that provides

    A   amusements   B   instructions

    C   facts   D   warnings

2. Prawns are similar to insects because they both

    A   have hard outer shells

    B   have six legs

    C   live in colonies

    D   can walk on the surface of water

3. Most insects start life as

    A   adults   B   spiders   C   cocoons   D   eggs

4. As used in the text the word *typical* means

    A   living in colonies   B   dangerous

    C   having special features   D   with similar qualities

5. The antenna of an ant is attached to its

    A   head   B   thorax   C   abdomen   D   legs

6. What important information does the writer have for the reader?

    A   Insects have a bad smell.

    B   The water strider cocoon produces silk.

    C   Insects are defenceless against other animals.

    D   Spiders are not insects.

7. How many body parts does an insect have?

Write your answer on the line. _____

8. Which of these insect types live in a social environment?

    A   mosquitoes   B   water striders   C   termites   D   cicadas

Need to try another report? Check the contents page.

Lit Tip 8 – Improve your literacy skills   **Full stops with titles**

Full stops are used at the end of sentences and for shortened titles.

If the last letter of a title is included no full stop is required, e.g. Dr for Doctor.

  Compare: Capt. for Captain and Mr for Mister.

Street signs no longer use a full stop for any shortened words, e.g. Dr for Drive.

Which of these words should have a full stop? Circle a number.

1. Hwy (Highway)   **2.** Br (Brother)   **3.** The Hon (The Honourable Bill Blogs)

4. Jr (Junior)   **5.** St (Saint Michael) **6.** Dep (Deputy Sanders)

Write the short form for; Senator _____ ,   Professor _____

Remember: Some titles are not shortened; included are Sir, Lord, and Miss.

Understanding Year 4 Comprehension
A. Horsfield © Five Senses Education © W. Marlin

Read the narrative *Library Rules.*

Library Rules

At her old school Alicia loved to borrow books. It had been fun. She had been a library monitor too. She would ask Mr Stone if she could become a monitor at the Grey Mansion School.

Inside children went about their work. Alicia queued up with Holly behind a short boy who fidgeted. A clock high on the wall showed the correct time – 1:25.

"I know why you're worried Billy, so stop wriggling like a worm," said the librarian.

"Yes, Mr Stone," mumbled Billy, shuffling forward.

Alicia looked at the signs behind the librarian's desk.

FINES PAID HERE

SILENCE IS GOLDEN	OVERDUE BOOKS WILL BE CHARGED $2 PER DAY
QUEUE BEHIND THE YELLOW LINE UNTIL CALLED	NO BORROWING AFTER 3:45

'Step forward Billy Page. What is your excuse for not having your book? It is now twenty-one days overdue.'

'I'm sure I returned it Mr Stone.'

'Are you suggesting I lost it? I have not seen *Dangerous Rescue* since it left this counter.'

'No Mr . . . .'

'No borrowing for you until the book is returned, or the fine paid, along with the cost of the book. A total of $54. Your parents will be informed. Next. Step forward.'

Billy shuffled away.

'I'm Alicia. I'm new. I would like to be a monitor, Mr Stone,' said Alicia politely.

'Grade 4 cannot be monitors.'

Alicia was dismayed.

'Holly, show Alicia around the library and explain the rules to her. Quietly.' said Mr Stone.

Holly took Alicia's hand and guided her way from the desk. Alicia wanted explanations but Holly shook her head cautiously.

Understanding Narratives   Circle a letter or write an answer for questions 1 to 8.

1. Who had to show Alicia around the library?
    A   Mr Stone   B   Billy Page   C   a monitor   D   Holly

2. What did Alicia most want from her visit to the library?
    A   to meet Mr Stone   B   to get permission to be a library monitor
    C   to borrow some books   D   to see how the library was organised

3. Mr Stone could be described as being
    A   stern   B   realistic   C   encouraging   D   disorganised

4. Billy Page was in trouble because he
    A   didn't have enough money for a fine   B   couldn't keep still in the queue
    C   had taken a book off the library counter D   hadn't returned a library book on time

5. What would happen if Billy Page did **not** pay the fine?
    A   he wouldn't be allowed to borrow any books
    B   he would have to wait in the queue
    C   he would have buy a copy of *Dangerous Rescue*
    D   he wouldn't be allowed in the library

6. Choose the word that best completes the following sentence.
    Billy Page was feeling _____ as he approached the library desk.

    A   happy   B   bothered   C   relaxed   D   neglected

7. How did Alicia know she had to be quiet in the library?
    A   Holly told her the rule
    B   Mr Stone announced the rule to the class
    C   Holly didn't speak to her as they left the library counter
    D   she saw a sign behind Mr Stone's desk

8. Write the numbers 1 to 4 in the boxes to show the correct order in which events occurred in the library. The first one (1) has been done for you.

1	Alicia enters the school library.
	Holly shows Alicia around the library.
	Alicia tells Mr Stone she would like to be a monitor.
	Alicia and Holly join a library queue.

Need to try another narrative passage? Check the contents page.

Lit Tip 9 – Improve your literacy skills   **The prefix *dis***

Dis is a prefix which most often means not. Disloyal means **not** loyal.

A person that has a dis<u>ease</u> is **not** at <u>ease</u>. They feel uncomfortable.

A person that is dissatisfied is **not** satisfied with something.

If something is **not** being used anymore it is in disuse.

What word would you use to describe:

a person: 1 who is **not** honest? _____ 2 who is **not** able _____

something: 3 you do **not** believe? _____ 4 you do **not** like _____

Understanding Year 4 Comprehension
A. Horsfield © Five Senses Education © W. Marlin

Sheep, Sheep, Come Home

This is an old English game and is played in many places across the world. Players will need a large outdoor area such as a playground or park or it can be played inside such places as a school gym, but it's more fun as an outside game that has borders on either side that don't let the players stray out of the games area.

This game becomes a mixture of screams or squeals of fear and delight that show the excitement of the players.

A child is chosen to be the shepherd. The shepherd herds his sheep to one end of the play area and he retreats to the other end. The wolf 'hides' in some corner between the sheep and the shepherd.

The shepherd then calls, 'Sheep, sheep, come home.'

The sheep reply, 'We can't. We are afraid.'

The shepherd then cries, 'What are you afraid of?'

The sheep call, 'The wolf!'

The shepherd then says, 'The wolf has gone to Devonshire (an English town) and won't be back for seven years. Sheep, sheep, come home.'

The sheep suddenly start to run to the shepherd at the other end of the playground.

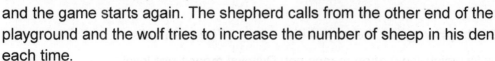

The wolf suddenly appears and chases the sheep until he catches one. Sometimes, the sheep are put in his den and the game starts again. The shepherd calls from the other end of the playground and the wolf tries to increase the number of sheep in his den each time.

In some games the wolf makes the sheep help him catch the other sheep. The game ends faster if this is done.

English villages often had their own interpretation of the game – often only a slight difference in words or actions, but enough to underline and add variety.

Adapted from: http://www.mkheritage.co.uk/sga/games/chasing-games.html

Understanding Procedures   Circle a letter to answer questions 1 to 8.

1. It is best if the game 'Sheep, sheep, come home', is played with
    - A   one player
    - B   two players
    - C   three players
    - D   many players

2. When do the sheep run to the shepherd?
    - A   when the wolf is not looking
    - B   when the wolf is near the shepherd
    - C   when the shepherd tells them to run
    - D   when the wolf cannot be seen

3. For the sheep, the game 'Sheep, sheep, come home' would be
    - A   exciting
    - B   dangerous
    - C   relaxing
    - D   refreshing

4. According to the text which statement is TRUE?
    - A   'Sheep, sheep, come home', is a boys' game.
    - B   Some sheep sometimes help the wolf catch other sheep.
    - C   The shepherd is the last person to get caught.
    - D   The wolf eats any sheep he catches.

5. The word 'hides' is written with quotation marks ('hides'). This means
    - A   the wolf cannot be seen
    - B   the players don't know where he is
    - C   the wolf is not really hiding
    - D   the shepherd doesn't know where the wolf is

6. What happens as soon as the shepherd first calls, 'Sheep, sheep, come home'?
    - A   the wolf hides in a corner of the play area
    - B   the wolf starts chasing the sheep
    - C   the sheep start running towards the shepherd
    - D   the sheep tell the shepherd that they are afraid

7. The word *enrich* in the last paragraph has a similar meaning to
    - A   improve   B   recharge   C   finish   D   spoil

8. The children in the picture are most likely
    - A   looking for where the wolf hides
    - B   escaping from the wolf's den
    - C   trying to reach Devonshire
    - D   racing to the shepherd's end of the field

Need to try another procedure passage? Check the contents page.

Lit Tip 10 – Improve your literacy skills   apostrophes for shortened words

An apostrophe is a punctuation mark that looks like this: '

We use the apostrophe to show that a letter (or letters) is missing in a contracted word (a contraction), that is, when we shorten two words after we join them together.

Examples: I'm = I am. The apostrophe shows where the missing letter (a) was placed.

Write the two words for these contractions. he's _____ , you're _____

What letters have been replaced by the apostrophe in: it's _____ , I've _____,

we're _____ , who's _____ , haven't _____ , don't _____ , I'll _____

Understanding Year 4 Comprehension
A. Horsfield © Five Senses Education © W. Marlin

Read the text and look at the pictures for *Comics and Cartoons*.

Comics and Cartoons

Comics aren't just for children, as some people might think. There are many comics written with adults in mind, and this is reflected in the style of the artwork. Comics are read all around the world in newspapers, in magazines, in books and on the internet. Some are created simply to make people chuckle, some are made for enjoyment (often with storylines as good as any novel) and there are some that make a comment on what is happening in society. Indeed, graphic novels are a very popular genre.

Comic strips - those made up of frames - have a surprisingly long and interesting history. For instance, there's evidence of comics in China from as long ago as the 11th century BC! That's about 10 000 years ago! Comics have <u>evolved</u> over the years with advances in technology and the changing styles of art and graphic art or cartoons, and are often at the <u>cutting edge</u> of design.

Understanding Comics and Cartoons Circle a letter or write an answer for questions 1 to 8.

1. Look at cartoon number ☐1☐. What do Santa's comments suggest?

    A   Santa doesn't know much about electronics.
    B   Santa won't give the boy any presents.
    C   Santa thinks the boy is being cheeky.
    D   Santa is tired of being asked questions.

2. Cartoon ☐1☐ is a very short comic strip. How many frames have been used?
   Write your answer in the box. ☐

3. Which word could be used instead of *evolved* as it is used in the text?
    A   grown   B   suffered   C   changed   D   endured

4. Look at cartoon number ☐2☐. The illustration suggests that the man is

    A   having a dream   B   waiting to get into heaven
    C   lost in a cloudy place   D   sitting up in bed

5. Comics and cartoons can often be found
    A   in school reports   B   on city buses
    C   in advertising flyers   D   on the internet

6. Look at cartoon number ☐2☐. The man's comments suggests he

    A   has had a very active life   B   understands the value of tweeting
    C   has wasted his time   D   still has some people to tweet

7. According to the text
    A   adults don't read comics   B   comics have a long history
    C   cartoons are better than comics D   all cartoons and comics are fun

8. Comics are often at the *cutting edge* of design. This suggests some comics
    A   are dangerous   B   use the latest techniques
    C   make people laugh   D   must be handled carefully

Lit Tip 11 – Improve your literacy skills   apostrophes s ('s) for ownership

Apostrophe s ('s) for ownership (or possession) is quite simple for singular nouns. You simply add 's to the noun. Girl is a singular noun, so we would write girl's hat to show that the girl owns a hat. If the girl were Wendy we would write Wendy's hat.

Even when the singular noun ends with an s we still add apostrophe s ('s): bus's door.

1. Add the apostrophe s (') to show ownership for these nouns.

    man ____ watch,   Dad ____ lunch   monkey ____ tail,   box ____ lid,   Justin ____ work

Wendy's hat can be written the hat of Wendy and no apostrophe s is required.

2. Write the tiger's claw without using an apostrophe of possession.

_____

Understanding Year 4 Comprehension
A. Horsfield © Five Senses Education © W. Marlin

Mr Tom Narrow

A scandalous man
Was Mr Tom Narrow!
He pushed his grandmother
Round in a barrow.
And he called out loud
As he rang his bell,
"Grannies to sell!
Old Grannies to sell!"

The neighbours said
As he passed them by,
"This poor old lady
We will not buy,
He surely must be
A mischievous man
To try to sell
His own dear Gran!"

"Besides," said another,
"if you ask me,
She'd be very small use
That I can see."
"You're right,' said a third,
"And no mistake -
A very poor bargain
she'd surely make."

So Mr Tom Narrow
He scratched his head,
And he sent his grandmother
Back to <u>bed</u>;
And he rang his bell
Through all the town
Till he sold his barrow
For half a crown*.

(*about 50 cents)

James Reeves (1909–1978)

Understanding Poetry   Circle a letter or tick a box to answer questions 1 to 8.

1. What was Mr Tom Narrow first trying to sell?
   - A   a barrow
   - B   his grandmother
   - C   a neighbour
   - D   his bell

2. The neighbours thought Mr Tom Narrow was
   - A   an inconsiderate man
   - B   a clever man
   - C   a nasty, cruel man
   - D   a careless man

3. The poem is most likely meant to be
   - A   a warning for grandmothers
   - B   a record of how things once were
   - C   an example of an advertisement
   - D   an entertaining read

4. Why was the third neighbour **not** interested in buying Mr Tom Narrow's granny?
   The third neighbour thought the granny
   - A   would be useless
   - B   was the wrong size
   - C   was much too dear
   - D   should not be for sale

5. What did Mr Tom Narrow finally do with his granny?
   - A   sold her with the barrow
   - B   got her to ring his bell
   - C   sent her back to bed
   - D   gave her away

6. When Mr Tom Narrow scratched his head (last stanza) it suggests he
   - A   had an itchy head
   - B   didn't know what to do
   - C   was pretending to think
   - D   upset by the neighbours

7. What word does the poet use to rhyme with *bed* (last stanza)?
   - A   bell
   - B   town
   - C   head
   - D   crown

8. Tick a box for TRUE or FALSE for this statement.
   The three neighbours were really upset by Mr Tom Narrow's treatment of his granny.

   TRUE ☐   FALSE ☐

Need to try another poem? Check the contents page.

Understanding Year 4 Comprehension
A. Horsfield © Five Senses Education © W. Marlin

What is an Adverb?

An adverb is a word that adds meaning to a verb. Verbs are often called doing words.

Adverbs usually follow a verb.

Look at this sentence: We saw the captain walk **slowly** to his boat.

The verb is walk. The adverb is **slowly**. It tells the reader how the captain walked.

We could use any of a variety of different adverbs for this sentence. They all change the meaning slightly.

> We saw the captain walk **quickly** to his boat.
> We saw the captain walk **silently** to his boat.
> We saw the captain walk **briskly** to his boat.

What did you notice about all the adverbs used? These adverbs all ended with *ly*.

These are the easiest adverbs to recognise. The suffix, ly, is a very common ending for adverbs.

Here are some others: happily, strangely, dangerously, fairly, suddenly, sadly, softly.

These adverbs tell **how** something is done.

Other adverbs may tell **when** something is done.

> The train arrived **late**.
> The baby will be asleep **soon**.

These examples do **not** end with *ly*.

Other adverbs may tell **where** something is done.

> The mail is in **here**.
> You should stand over **there**.

These examples do **not** end with *ly*.

Remember: some **when** and **where** adverbs may end in *ly*.

When Jason walked down the street he saw this sign:

Jason knew there was a mistake in the sign. Can you pick the mistake?

Of course, some words that end with *ly* are not adverbs. Jelly is a noun!

Remember: Just as adjectives improve nouns, adverbs improve verbs. They add extra meaning.

Understanding Explanations   Circle a letter or write an answer for questions 1 to 8.

1. How many types of adverbs does the text describe?
      A   one   B   two   C   three   D   four

2. Choose the word that is **not** an adverb.
      A   silly   B   truly   C   strangely   D   madly

3. In which word did Jason see the mistake?
      A   work   B   progress   C   dive   D   slow

4. A word is missing in this sentence. Jodi wrote _____ in her workbook.
    Which would be the correct word to complete the sentence?
      A   careful   B   carefuller   C   carefully   D   caring

5. Complete this sentence with an adverb that ends with *ly*.

    The boys cheered _____ during the football final. (Answers will vary.)

6. Which sentence does **not** have a mistake?
      A   Justin walked quick through the shop.
      B   The rain fell heavily all night.
      C   The choir sang happy at the concert.
      D   It all happened so sudden that I was scared.

7. Choose the word that is an adverb.
      A   lightly   B   billy   C   holy   D   butterfly

8. Which word is an example of an adverb telling **where** something happened?
      A   here   B   smoothly   C   lazily   D   late

Need to try another explanation passage? Check the contents page.

Lit Tip 13 – Improve your literacy skills   What is tense?

The tense of a verb tells you when the action happens.

There are three main simple tenses: **present**, **past** and **future**.

Things to know about simple tense: Present tense uses the basic form of the verb.

Past tense verbs have a few patterns.

Future tense need <u>will</u> (shall) + the verb.

Look at the verb cook: I cook my supper every night. (present tense)

I cook<u>ed</u> our dinner yesterday. (past tense)

I <u>will cook</u> breakfast tomorrow. (future tense)

What is the tense of these sentences?

I play my match right now! _____ tense

I played a match last year. _____ tense

I will play a match next season. _____ tense

Understanding Year 4 Comprehension
A. Horsfield © Five Senses Education © W. Marlin

Sending Parcels

Over recent years there has been a decrease in 'snail' mail and an increase in parcel post, mainly because of an increase in internet shopping. There is more competition among couriers for delivery services. Australia Post has come up with friendly ways to make sending a parcel very simple.

Australia Post uses the catch phrase: *Simple* as 1, 2, 3.

1. At the Post Shop you choose the speed you want your parcel delivered. On a stand find the envelope that suits your needs. The quicker the delivery the dearer the cost.

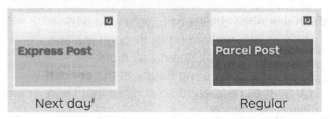

Next day Express Post mainly applies to major cities. To country areas delivery may take a little longer.

2. Make sure you have an envelope the right weight size for your contents.
    Using the weight maximums given as shown below, the heavier the contents the dearer the delivery cost.

3. If you need to know if your parcel arrives at its destination you can:
    *   pay extra to ensure against loss or damage to the parcel. This is recommended when sending valuable items.
    *   have the addressees sign for the parcel on delivery. This is recommended for important documents.

Now all you have to do is pay for and then address the envelope and drop into a letterbox.

Express Post parcels go into a yellow letterbox. Regular Post parcels go into a red letterbox – or you can leave your parcel with the friendly officer behind the counter in the Post Shop. Australia Post will do the rest!

Understanding Procedures   Circle a letter or write an answer for questions 1 to 8.

1. What do the numbers, 1, 2 and 3 stand for?
    A   the types of envelope available
    B   the steps needed to send a parcel
    C   the different weights of envelopes available
    D   the days it takes to make a delivery

2. I have a parcel that weighs 400g. The cost will be
    A   less than for a 500g envelope
    B   the same as for 500g parcel
    C   the same price as a 3kg parcel
    D   decided by the Post Office staff

3. If I want a parcel delivered as fast as possible what type of envelope should I buy?

    Write your answer on the line._____

4. Which statement is CORRECT?
    A   Internet shopping has created an increase in parcel deliveries.
    B   Express parcels should be placed in the red letterbox for delivery.
    C   Post Office staff cannot help customers with information.
    D   All Express Post deliveries must be signed for.

5. What is the last thing a person does before a parcel can be delivered?
    A   pays for the envelope
    B   writes an address on the envelope
    C   talks to the officer at the Post Shop counter
    D   puts the envelope in the correct letterbox

6. The Australia Post uses a *catch phrase*. A catch phrase
    A   uses words taken from a song
    B   is a trick to get a customer to buy something
    C   is a well-known saying
    D   has words you cannot forget

7. The word *regular* as used to describe certain types of delivery service could be replaced with the synonym
    A   ordinary   B   constant   C   repeated   D   official

8. This information would most likely be displayed
    A   at a newsagent
    B   on a courier's van
    C   at a Post Shop
    D   in TV advertising

Need to try another procedure passage? Check the contents page.

Lit Tip 14 – Improve your literacy skills   Regular verbs

A regular verb is a verb that forms its past tense (and past participle) by adding the suffix *ed* to the verb.

Examples: walk/walked, play/played, cry/cried, use/used, pat/patted

The majority of English verbs are called regular verbs. Sometimes there are rules to follow when the suffix is added.

Write the past tense of these regular verbs; jump _____ , toss _____ , try _____ ,
skip _____ , copy _____ , trace _____

Understanding Year 4 Comprehension
A. Horsfield © Five Senses Education © W. Marlin

Read a Real Book!

Children are now reading fewer novels whether they are hard copies or ebooks. The trend has been to read lots of short matter such as blogs and texts and give the longer reading material a miss. If you want to improve your brain you might think about becoming a bookworm.

Reading exposes people to a wider range of words and ideas making them better communicators. A person's vocabulary increases the more they read books.

Unlike blog posts and news articles, sitting down with a book takes long periods of concentration, which is hard to do at first. Being fully absorbed in a book involves shutting out the outside word and getting involved in the text. This can strengthen your <u>attention span</u>.

People are only limited by what can be imagined and from the worlds described in books, both fiction and non-fiction. This helps readers expand their understanding of what is possible. Through reading, the mind creates an image in the head, instead of having the image given to them when they watch a film.

Real books offer a wealth of learning and is easier and much cheaper than going to school. Reading gives you a chance to learn a lot in a short time.

Finally, reading reduces stress. People only need to read silently for six minutes to slow down the heart rate and ease tension in the muscles. It gets the subject's stress level lower than before they started.

Of all a book's benefits its greatest is its entertainment value. Reading is better than watching a TV show - a good book can keep you amused while developing life skills.

Adapted from: http://whytoread.com/why-to-read-10-reasons-why-reading-will-save-your-life/

"The reading of good books is like conversation with the finest men of past centuries."

Descartes.

Understanding Persuasions   Circle a letter or write an answer for questions 1 to 8.

1. The text is trying to convince readers to
    A   buy hard-cover books   B   read longer text
    C   watch better TV shows   D   read fewer news articles

2. According to the text, the greatest benefit of reading a book is
    A   being entertained by the text   B   learning to use new words
    C   a better understanding of blogs   D   improved education

3. One word in the first paragraph is a compound word. What is that word?

    Write your answer on the line._____

4. The writer suggests that to slow down a rapid heart-rate people should
    A   read less ebooks
    B   increase the number of words they use
    C   watch amusing TV shows
    D   read silently for six minutes

5. Which idea from the text is an opinion and **NOT** a fact?
    A   Reading is not only fun, it has other benefits.
    B   Children are now reading fewer novels.
    C   Reading gives you a chance to learn a lot.
    D   Sitting down with a book takes long periods of concentration.

6. A person's *attention span* refers to the length of time
    A   one can maintain silence   B   necessary to understand a text
    C   someone can concentrate   D   a person can use their imagination

7. Which word from the text has the opposite meaning to disadvantage?
    A   miss   B   image   C   benefit   D   trend

8. To improve their imagination a person should
    A   read more books   B   be less stressed
    C   buy cheap books   D   go to school

Need to try another persuasion passage? Check the contents page.

Lit Tip 15 – Improve your literacy skills   Irregular verbs

Verbs in English are called irregular verbs if they don't have the conventional ed suffix, (such as in asked or ended) to make the past tense.

Examples: write/wrote, sing/sang, draw/drew, know/knew, sweep/swept

Write the past tense of these irregular verbs; eat _____ , speak _____ , see _____, blow _____ , buy _____ , say _____

Can you add the correct form of the verb forget to this sentences?

Gosh! It's raining and I have _____ my umbrella.

Understanding Year 4 Comprehension
A. Horsfield © Five Senses Education © W. Marlin

Lost Time

I didn't know it at the time but it all started one Saturday when I walked into the kitchen.

Mum was gazing out the window with an odd look on her face.

'I've been here all morning and I have lost a whole hour,' she complained as she absently watched Mr Grimm make his way up the street.

Mr Grimm is new in our neighbourhood. He's an older man who wears odd clothes. His long, grey flowing coat goes right down to the ground. It has a rather large hood that hides his face. His outfit looks a thousand years old. Should get a new one. Better still, should get something modern, I thought!

Dad walked in. Must have heard Mum's complaint. 'I just saved ten minutes mowing the front lawn.' he said smugly.

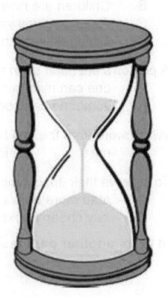

Quick as a flash I cheekily asked, 'Where?'

Dad thought I was serious! 'Annie', he replied as if I had asked a dumb question, 'I put them in a jar by the lawn.'

I frowned and squinted, but he was serious. I trundled across the veranda and out onto the lawn to see these 'saved ten minutes in a jar'. Should've been in an hourglass I reckoned smugly.

As I expected there was nothing there. I immediately told Dad!

Did that get a reaction? It did! Dad was out to the lawn like a bolt of dizzy lightning.

'It's gone!' he yelled. 'The ten minutes I saved have been lost.'

'Maybe stolen?' I joked.

He glared at me! 'Really!'

'I'll just have to make up time,' he muttered gloomily.

'Why not find the lost ones?' I perked teasingly.

'What if it's been taken out the jar?' Dad shot back. 'I'd never recognise it.'

Understanding Narratives   Circle a letter for questions 1 to 8.

1. Where was the narrator's mother when she saw Mr Grimm?
   - A   in the street
   - B   on the front lawn
   - C   in the kitchen
   - D   on the veranda

2. What did Annie find unusual about Mr Grimm?
   - A   He wore strange clothes.
   - B   He stole people's saved time.
   - C   He wandered the streets.
   - D   He went into the kitchen.

3. The text states Annie: *frowned and squinted.*
   This suggests that Annie was
   - A   hard of hearing
   - B   doubting what she had been told
   - C   trying to be serious
   - D   suffering in the sunlight

4. What did Annie's father do when he was told about the missing jar of time?
   - A   He went after Mr Grimm.
   - B   He rushed out to the front lawn.
   - C   He thought Annie was joking.
   - D   He looked for an hour glass.

5. What did Annie suggest could be done about her father's lost jar of time?
   - A   They could asked Mr Grimm for it.
   - B   They should check to see if it had been split.
   - C   They should find who stole the jar.
   - D   They should conduct a search for the jar.

6. Which words from the text are an example of a simile?
   - A   Mum was gazing out the window with an odd look on her face.
   - B   His long, grey flowing coat goes right down to the ground.
   - C   Quick as a flash I cheekily asked, 'Where?'
   - D   As I expected there was nothing there.

7. The saving of time, as Annie understood the idea, could best be described as
   - A   practical   B   common   C   important   D   ridiculous

8. What was Annie's father expecting to be found in the garden?
   - A   a jar of saved time
   - B   the visitor, Mr Grimm
   - C   an hour glass
   - D   his lawn mower

Need to try another narrative passage? Check the contents page.

Lit Tip 16 – Improve your literacy skills   Proper nouns

Nouns are naming words. Nouns name people, places and things. Every noun can be further classified as **common** or **proper**. A common noun names general items.

Examples: table, chair, phone, cup, fan.

Proper nouns name specific people, places or things, and require a capital.

Examples: Peter, Queen Elizabeth, Darwin, Easter, Mt Tomah, Toyota, Glenelg, Myer.

Circle the proper nouns.   Einstein   oven   fear   Tasmania   Bill   carrot

Write a proper noun for these common nouns.   city _____ , dog _____ , lake _____ ,
friend _____ , shop _____ , team _____

(Note: answers will vary but all must have capital letters.)

Understanding Year 4 Comprehension
A. Horsfield © Five Senses Education © W. Marlin

Sandcastles and Sand Sculptures

Of course you know how to build a sand castle! It's such an easy task and only requires a cheap, little plastic bucket and spade to make a start. The blade of the spade should have a smooth face to make digging easier.

The beach is the perfect spot for sandcastles but a sand pit could work just as well – for a practice!

Damp sand doesn't stay stuck together very well. Water is required. Water will turn the damp sand into a stickier substance. The moisture in the sand is very important when building a castle. If it's too dry, the sand grains will separate and the castle will collapse. If the sand is too wet, the castle will buckle under its own weight.

Fill your bucket with sand then upturn it suddenly on the beach. Gently lift the bucket up and you should have the first piece of your castle. To build the base dump buckets of sand into a square or circular shape. <u>Fashion</u> this shape from the castle walls.

Now, all you really need to know is how the finished castle will appear. Keep piling up the wet sand like bricks, smoothing out edges as you go. <u>Work</u> from the bottom to the top. You can add towers, steps and windows or add some seashells, or other bits you find nearby. Blow away excess sand using a straw.

Photo: A. Horsfield

Sand sculpturing is not only for kids.

This dragon is nearing completion. Black stones give texture to its hide. Candles in its nose holes make it look as if it could breathe fire!

If onlookers like the sculptor's creation they can drop a coin into his tip tin.

Source: http://www.kidzworld.com/article/4549-summer-fun-building-sand-castles
http://www.redbookmag.com/kids-family/cute-kid-contest/sand-castle-building-tips#slide-1

Understanding Explanations   Circle a letter or write an answer for questions 1 to 8.

1. Building sandcastles
   A   is a well paid activity
   B   is simpler than sand sculpturing
   C   involves a lot of spare time
   D   requires the skill of an adult

2. What is the most important feature of the spade used in building a sandcastle?
   A   the material spade is made from
   B   the size of the blade
   C   the strength of the handle
   D   the surface of the blade

3. The word *work* as used in paragraph 5 in the text is a
   A   adjective   B   verb   C   adverb   D   noun

4. The problem with some sand when building a sandcastle is the
   A   colour of the sand
   B   speed at which the sand dries
   C   wetness of the sand
   D   additional candles and matches

5. What is the sculptor's tip tin used for?
   A   money donations
   B   a handy supply of extra sand
   C   spare water to wet the sand
   D   additional candles and matches

6. According to the text, which statement is TRUE.
   A   Building with sand is strictly a child's activity.
   B   Straws can be used to make castle towers.
   C   Many buckets of sand are required to build a sandcastle.
   D   To build a sandcastle the first attempts should be in a sand pit.

7. Write the numbers 1 to 4 in the boxes to show the correct order in which things are done when building a sandcastle The first one (1) has been done for you.

	Fill the bucket with sand.
1	Make sure the sand is moist enough.
	Make the castle sides smooth.
	Dump buckets of sand to make the castle base.

8. Which word is a synonym for *fashion* in paragraph 4 as used in the text
   A   mould   B   method   C   carve   D   clothes

Need to try another explanation? Check the contents page.

Understanding Year 4 Comprehension
A. Horsfield © Five Senses Education © W. Marlin

Read the lyrics of the song *Teddy Bears' Picnic*.

The music was written in 1907. The lyrics were added in 1932.
It was first recorded by Henry Hall in 1932. Since then it has been widely recorded and the music used in TV series, commercials and films, the first being in 1926. The tune was used in an Audi car commercial in 2011.

Teddy Bears' Picnic

If you go down in the woods today you're sure of a big surprise,
If you go down in the woods today you'd better go in disguise.
For every bear that there was will gather there for certain because.
Today's the day the Teddy Bears have their picnic.

Every Teddy Bear who's been good is sure of a treat today.
There's lot of marvellous things to eat and wonderful games to play.
Beneath the trees where nobody sees they'll hide and seek as long as they please.
That's the way the Teddy Bears have their picnic.

Picnic time for Teddy Bears,
The little Teddy Bears are having a lovely time today.
Watch them, catch them unawares and see them picnic on their holiday.
See them gaily gad about.
They love to play and shout.
They never have any care.
At six o'clock their Mummies and Daddies will take them home to bed
'Cause they're tired little Teddy Bears.

(Repeat chorus)
If you go down in the woods today you're sure of a big surprise,
If you go down in the woods today you'd better go in disguise
For every bear that ever there was will gather there for certain because
Today's the day the Teddy Bears have their picnic.

Songwriters: J W Bratton and J Kennedy

Understanding Song lyrics   Circle a letter or write an answer for questions 1 to 8.

1. The lyrics of a song refer to its
   A   words   B   tune   C   notes   D   title

2. The Teddy Bears were taken home at six o'clock because
   A   their Mummies and Daddies were tired
   B   they were exhausted from playing games
   C   they saw someone in the woods
   D   they were going to go on a picnic

3. The word *gad* as used in the text (line 12) means to
   A   feel dizzy   B   they had a rest
   C   run about happily   D   they ate their picnic food

4. What the Teddy Bears do under the trees?
   A   they enjoyed a treat   B   they had a rest
   C   they played hide and seek   D   they ate their picnic food

5. The writer has used the word's '*Cause* (line 26). What is '*Cause* short for?

   Write the word on the line._____

6. If someone wanted to see the Teddy Bears having a picnic they should
   A   hide beneath the trees   B   alter their appearance
   C   join in the Teddy Bears' games   D   wait in the woods

7. When was the music of the Teddy Bears' Picnic first used in a film?
   A   1907   B   1932   C   1926   D   2011

8. What is the most likely reason the Teddy Bears are having a picnic?
   A   the day of the picnic was a holiday   B   it was one of the bear's birthday
   C   it was a lovely day for a picnic   D   a reward for being good

---

Lit Tip 18 – Improve your literacy skills   **Person (or point of view)**

Person in story writing refers to how the story is told, or who the text is meant for. There are three approaches to text: we use the terms first, second or third person. The use of first, second or third person creates the way the reader reacts to the writing.

Writing in **first person** the writer uses personal pronouns I, we, me and us. The text may also may include such words as my, mine and our. The narrator in the first person text talks about himself/herself.

Second person text uses you as well as your. The writer speaks directly to the reader.

Third person text includes such pronouns as he, she, it, they and them.

Many books you read are written in first or third person.

Write the letters F for first, S for second and T for third in the boxes to show the person these sentences are in.

You are just a silly boy! ☐   Jack walked quickly towards the office. ☐

I heard the wind in the trees. ☐   The car came around the corner. ☐

Understanding Year 4 Comprehension
A. Horsfield © Five Senses Education © W. Marlin

The Bermuda Triangle

The story of disappearing bomber planes is one of the more puzzling mysteries of the Atlantic Ocean. 5 December 1945, was a clear, sunny day. Early that day a routine flying exercise had been planned for pilots at the air force base in Florida (USA).

At 2 o'clock in the afternoon five Avenger bombers took off in an easterly direction over the Atlantic heading towards the Bahamas (islands east of Florida) for a *mock torpedo attack* on a target ship.

These massive single-engine bombers were among the largest and the most powerful ever built at that time. Each aircraft had a crew of three.

The first sign of the unusual happening came at 3:45 pm, just fifteen minutes before the planes were due back to base. A frantic message came over the radio when the pilot announced that they seemed to be off course and couldn't see land. Worse was to follow. They didn't know their position.

The controller at the base was amazed. He ordered the planes to fly due west. The planes reported back that they didn't know which way was west!

The following message from the planes trailed off as the navigator reported, "We don't know where we are. The ocean doesn't look as it should. We are entering white water!"

Nothing more was heard. The five bombers simply disappeared. Searches were immediately launched and in the course of the search a flying boat disappeared near the last known position of the five bombers. No wreckage, no oil slicks, no bodies, no life-rafts were found.

The area of the disappearance became known as the Bermuda Triangle. Since then there have been other unexplained happenings in the area.

Understanding Recounts   Circle a letter or write an answer for questions 1 to 8.

1. The recount tells the events of
    A   a successful torpedo attack   B   a misunderstanding
    C   an exciting rescue attempt   D   an unsolved mystery

2. What is meant by a *mock torpedo attack*?
    A   an attack that was a practice exercise
    B   a military exercise that humiliated the enemy
    C   a surprise attack in full daylight
    D   an exercise where the destination is unknown

3. What direction is San Juan in Puerto Rico from Bermuda?
    A   north   B   south   C   east   D   west

4. What fact first amazed the flight controller in Miami?
    A   The bombers had been warned to keep out of the Bermuda Triangle.
    B   He had to send out a flying boat to assist the bombers.
    C   The Avenger's crew had no idea which direction was west.
    D   Five powerful bombers were lost at sea on a fine day.

5. When was the base at Miami aware there could be a problem with the flight?
    A   early on the morning of 5 November 1945
    B   just after take-off at 2 o'clock in the afternoon
    C   when the flying boat crew failed to find wreckage
    D   15 minutes before the planes were due back to base

6. Write the numbers 1 to 4 in the boxes to show the correct order in which events occurred in the
    report. The first one (1) has been done for you.

1	The Avenger bombers take off from Florida.
	The rescue flying boat disappears.
	The navigator sends an urgent message to the base.
	The Avenger bomber crew lose sight of land.

7. In which direction did the Avenger bombers head after take-off?
    A   north   B   south   C   east   D   west

8. The Bermuda Triangle is mainly situated in the
    A   United States   B   Atlantic Ocean
    C   Gulf of Mexico   D   Caribbean Sea

Need to try another recount? Check the contents page.

Understanding Year 4 Comprehension
A. Horsfield © Five Senses Education © W. Marlin

Where's Wally? Hits a Major <u>Milestone</u>

Book sales now total over 60 million copies worldwide. *A major achievement for the character who is celebrating 25 years in 2013.*

Martin Handford is an English children's author and illustrator who gained worldwide fame in the mid-1980s with his book *Where's Wally?* (known in the United States and Canada as *Where's Waldo?*)

Twenty-five years ago, *Where's Wally?* kick-started a global publishing phenomenon. Many years and bestselling books later, Wally is more than just a beloved picture-puzzle book character, he has become a pop culture icon, and now has hit the major sales milestone of sixty million copies sold in what has become a banner birthday year.

New publishing including anniversary editions of the original books, as well as hugely successful travel editions have driven a massive sales boost for Wally across all major sales channels.

Wally facts and figures:

* *Where's Wally?* is a publishing sensation! More than **60** million copies have been sold worldwide, encompassing more than **32** languages in **38** countries.

* *Where's Wally?* held the record for the fastest - selling children's book of all time (until Harry Potter).

* *Where's Wally?* has been Number 1 on the *New York Times* bestsellers list three times.

* Wally has reached star status! He has appeared in the primetime TV shows *Frasier*, *The Simpsons*, and *Friends*, on the 1,000th issue cover of *Rolling Stone* magazine.

* Fans love to dress up as Wally. According to Guinness, the official world record for the largest gathering of people dressed as Wally was set at the Street Performance Word Championship in June 2011 - 3,872 people took to the streets of Dublin, Ireland, in a sea of red-and-white stripes.

Have you read and searched for Wally?

Sources: http://en.wikipedia.org/wiki/Where's_Wally%3F
    http://sharongreenawaysreviews.wordpress.com/2013/06/17/wheres-wallys-amazing-milestone/

Understanding Reports   Circle a letter or write an answer for questions 1 to 8.

1. How long have the *Where's Wally* books been in existence?
   A   25 years   B   32 years   C   38 years   D   60 years

2. *Where's Wally* is a type of
   A   adventure story   B   information book
   C   puzzle magazine   D   education text

3. The *Where's Wally* books have been published in
   A   three languages   B   thirty-two languages
   C   thirty-eight languages   D   sixty languages

4. As used in the title, the word *milestone* means
   A   a stone set up beside a road to show the distance from a certain place
   B   something that causes a stumble while trying to make progress
   C   an obstacle that prevents a person achieving of a goal
   D   an important stage in the history of a fictional character

5. The people of Ireland wore red and white stripes in 2011 Street Performance World Championship because
   A   red and white make a spectacular display for Street Performances
   B   the two colours make up the stripes on the clothes Wally wears
   C   it was a requirement of the Guinness Book of Records
   D   red and white are the national colours of Ireland

6. The character *Wally* has appeared on the front of the
   A   *Guinness Book of Records*   B   *New York Times* newspaper
   C   *Rolling Stone* magazine   D   *Harry Potter* books

7. Wally has a different name in some countries. What is that name?

   Write the word on the line._____

8. The author of *Where's Wally,* Martin Handford, lives in
   A   England   B   Canada
   C   Ireland   D   United States

Need to try another report? Check the contents page.

Lit Tip 20 – Improve your literacy skills   **Capitals for deity references**

The word deity refers to divine names in religions: God, Christ, Allah, Buddha, Christianity, Judaism, Jews, Islam. All these words have capitals.

Words directly connected to religions also have capitals: Holy Bible, Torah, Son of God, Heaven. Many of these words can be used as common nouns and do not require capitals.

   Dad says his copy of How to Garden is his <u>bible</u>!

   We saw statues of Roman <u>gods</u> all across Italy.

Tick the sentences that should have used capital letters for <u>sacred</u> words.

1. The trip through the city lights was a heavenly experience. ☐
2. The word of god is there for everyone to read. ☐
3. Mr Landa was late for church again! ☐
4. We should behave like christians all the time. ☐

Understanding Year 4 Comprehension
A. Horsfield © Five Senses Education © W. Marlin

Madeleine Says

Madeleine says,
The price of food is just too high;
El Niño's made the weather dry;
The emu once knew how to fly;
And babies shouldn't ever cry;
Madeleine says.

Madeleine says,
The clouds are full of acid rain;
It's much too slow to go by train;
That she could fly an aeroplane;
And women have a bigger brain;
Madeleine says.

Madeleine says,
Her father's getting her a car;
That she could bend an iron bar;
Last night she saw a shooting star;
And Venus isn't very far;
Madeleine says.

Madeleine says,
The world gets smaller every day;
When she grows up she'll write a play;
That black and white are sometimes grey;
And <u>global</u> warming's here to stay;
Madeleine says.

And Madeleine says,
One day she'll be Prime Minister.
And Madeleine knows!

Elaine Horsfield

Understanding Poetry   Circle a letter or write an answer for questions 1 to 8.

1. What does Madeleine say about global warming?
   - A   It will soon go away.
   - B   It will last forever.
   - C   Scientists do not understand it.
   - D   She will fix it when she becomes prime minister.

2. For Madeleine train travel is
   - A   much too slow
   - B   very dirty
   - C   not reliable
   - D   uncomfortable

3. What is the best punctuation mark to complete the following sentences?

   Madeleine says, "What if a cow didn't eat hay ☐

   - A   full stop, inverted commas (.")
   - B   inverted commas, question mark ("?)
   - C   comma, inverted commas (,")
   - D   question mark inverted commas (?")

4. Which of Madeleine's comments is about pollution?
   - A   The clouds are full of acid rain.
   - B   Black and white are sometimes grey.
   - C   Last night she saw a shooting star.
   - D   The world gets smaller every day.

5. Madeleine wants to do many things.
   Which of the following options is **not** one of Madeleine's ambitions?
   - A   to own a car
   - B   to bend an iron bar
   - C   to ride a shooting star
   - D   to write a play

6. What is one thing Madeline is certain about?
   - A   women have bigger brains
   - B   she will become Prime Minister
   - C   black and white are sometimes grey
   - D   babies should never cry

7. Which word best describes Madeleine?
   - A   confident   B   confused   C   concerned   D   crazy

8. The word *global* means
   - A   very important
   - B   huge and round
   - C   world wide
   - D   changeable weather

Need to try another poem? Check the contents page.

Lit Tip 21 – Improve your literacy skills   What are redundant words?

Redundant words are unnecessary words in sentences.

Look at this sentence. A <u>male</u> man was caught by the police.

The word male is redundant because all men are males! The word male can be left out and there is no change of meaning.

Underline the redundant word in each sentence.

1. We put frozen ice in our fruit juice.

2. Apples fell down from the tree.

3. The armed gunman was captured.

4. The lost ball could not be found.

Understanding Year 4 Comprehension
A. Horsfield © Five Senses Education © W. Marlin

Nasrudin's Choice

Nasrudin lived in a country far away from Australia. Every day he would go into the village market square and beg for money or food because he was very poor. The local stall holders would make fun of him. They would show him two coins, one worth a lot more than the other and ask Nasrudin to choose a coin to keep.

Nasrudin would always choose the one with much less value which he was allowed to keep.

Eventually the story went out around the whole <u>province</u> and day after day groups of men and women would show up to watch Nasrudin. People would come forward and show Nasrudin two coins of different values and he would always choose the coin of least value. The onlookers would laugh.

One day, a kind, generous trader, tired of seeing Nasrudin ridiculed in such a way, beckoned him over to a quiet corner in the square. Speaking softly he said, "When they offer you two coins, you should choose the larger one. That way you would get a lot more money and the people wouldn't consider you an idiot."

"That sounds like good advice," replied Nasrudin, "but if I chose the larger coin, people would stop offering me money, because they like to believe I am even more stupid than they are."

The kind man thought about this.

Nasrudin explained, "You've no idea how much money I'm given by using this trick. There is nothing wrong with looking like a fool if, in fact, you are really being very clever.

(Mulla Nasrudin is thought to be based on a Persian character, dating from the 1300s. The Nasrudin Tales have spread throughout the Middle East and are seen as stories and wisdom tales in the Sufi tradition. www.rodney@hebsion.com/JJmulla-nasrudin.htm

Understanding Folk Tales   Circle a letter or write an answer for questions 1 to 8.

1. Nasrudin went to the market square each day because he was

    A   lazy   B   tired   C   lonely   D   poor

2. The text is most like

    A   a narrative   B   a persuasive text

    C   a procedure   D   an explanation

3. According to the text which statement is CORRECT?

    A   Nasrudin knew he looked like a foolish person.

    B   The generous trader guessed what Nasrudin was doing.

    C   The stall holders found Nasrudin's behaviour an embarrassment.

    D   Nasrudin let the villagers know they were more stupid than he was.

4. Nasrudin's reputation was

    A   restricted to the market square   B   unknown among stall holders

    C   limited to visitors to the market   D   spreading to regions beyond his town

5. Write the numbers 1 to 4 in the boxes to show the correct order in which events occurred in the tale. The first one (1) has been done for you.

	A stallholder offers Nasrudin a choice of coins.
	The people laugh at Nasrudin's stupid choice.
	Nasrudin chooses the coin of lesser value.
1	Nasrudin went to the market square.

6. The trader who spoke to Nasrudin

    A   wanted a share of Nasrudin's money

    B   thought Nasrudin's trick was very funny

    C   wanted to protect Nasrudin from ridicule

    D   didn't approve of Nasrudin's scheme

7. The stallholders and the villagers thought Nasrudin was

    A   unfair   B   simple   C   smart   D   bold

8. What would happen if Nasrudin took the larger coin?

    A   He would get rich much faster.

    B   People would not offer him money anymore.

    C   The onlookers would get angry.

    D   The trader would take the money.

Lit Tip 22 – Improve your literacy skills   **Affixes, prefixes and suffixes**

An **affix** is any addition to a base word that modifies the word's meaning.

There are two main types of affixes: **prefixes** and **suffixes**.

A **prefix** is a letter or letters placed before a base word, e.g. <u>re</u>turns.

A **suffix** is a letter or letters placed at the end of a base word, e.g. turn<u>s</u>.

A base word can take a prefix and suffix, e.g. returns.

Some common prefixes are: un, re, pre. Examples: <u>un</u>happy, <u>re</u>wite, <u>pre</u>fix.

Some common suffixes are s, ed, ing, ful. Examples: day<u>s</u>, wait<u>ed</u>, eat<u>ing</u>, use<u>ful</u>.

Underline the affixes in these words.   hopeful   prepare   buses   trees

playing   quietly   bicycle   recall   suitable   uncooked

Understanding Year 4 Comprehension
A. Horsfield © Five Senses Education © W. Marlin

Energy In – Energy Out

Jellybeans, like any sweets, are made up with sugar.
Young people love the taste of sugar. People love
the instant energy sugar provides. But with anything,
moderation is the key. We need to balance the energy
inputs (what we eat) with our outputs (the energy we
use) while recognising the importance of taste (treats
we like) and nutrition (what's good for us).

People like sugar for taste and energy. Sugar is
important for providing the energy necessary for bodies
to function properly.

Sugar is a type of carbohydrate. Other carbohydrate-
rich foods include bread, cereal, fruit, rice, potatoes and
pasta. Carbohydrates are the body's preferred energy
source.

Sugar comes in three main forms: raw, brown and white.

During digestion, all sugars (and other carbohydrates) are broken down into
simple sugars, called glucose, which then travel through the blood stream to
body cells. There it provides energy or is stored as glycogens in our muscles or
in our liver for future use.

Since sugar has half the calories of fat – 1 teaspoon of sugar contains only 20
calories but 1 teaspoon of fat contain 45 calories. Sugar is less fattening.

With kind permission adapted from: *The journey of the jellybean* produced by Canegrowers

Understanding Reports   Circle a letter or write an answer for questions 1 to 8.

1. What does sugar provide for the human body?

   A   fat   B   fluids   C   warmth   D   energy

2. The text is trying to convince people to

   A   avoid eating too many sweets
   B   eat the same amount of sugar and fat
   C   choose only the foods they like
   D   eat more jelly beans

3. There is a compound word in the first paragraph.

   Write the word on this line._____

4. Which of these statements is a **fact** from the text?

   A   Carbohydrates are stored in our blood system.
   B   Sugar in your diet helps you to lose weight.
   C   Jellybeans are the best energy food for sportspeople.
   D   Fat has more calories than the same amount of sugar.

5. According to the text which of these is not listed as a source of carbohydrates?

   A   bread   B   potatoes   C   milk   D   rice

6. What is stored in our livers for future use?

   A   glycogens   B   brown sugar
   C   blood   D   raw sugar

7. Nutrition is described as being food that

   A   provides energy   B   has a nice taste
   C   is good for us   D   we eat by the spoonful

8. The text describes jellybeans as a

   A   fat   B   treat   C   cereal   D   fruit

Need to try another report? Check the contents page.

Understanding Year 4 Comprehension
A. Horsfield © Five Senses Education © W. Marlin

Meet Bruiser

Mitch's mother hurried in through the front door. 'Just met the neighbours. The Bulls,' she puffed. 'Nice family.'

Mitch looked up, startled. She had ventured alone, into enemy territory!

All Mitch could say was,'Oh.' Even the name, Bull, was a worry. Bulls were big and bulls were dangerous.

'They have two children. Di and Bruce,' beamed Mitch's mother.

'Bruce Bull the Bruiser.' muttered Mitch.

'You should go over and meet Bruce. You'll be in his class.' said Mitch's mother brightly.

Mitch's heart nearly stopped. He hadn't thought of that. 'Later Mum,' he managed to mumble.

'Whatever,' agreed his mother, 'but don't leave it too long. School tomorrow.'

Mitch shook his head as his mother hurried from the room. She still had the cartons to unpack.

Mitch's job was to stack the empty removalist's cartons in the backyard.

From his bedroom window Mitch watched Bruiser shifting rocks for their new rockery.

Rock after rock clunked into the barrow. The wheelbarrow shuddered every time! So did Mitch.

Makes his muscles strong, Mitch thought, still worried about school the next day and his new class. He suspected that Bruiser was the class bully. Bruiser Bull the Boss! And everyone knew that bullies always picked on new kids.

A ball flew over the fence landing behind the empty removalist cartons.

Mitch was about to retrieve it when a movement caught his eye. It was Bruiser, boldly peering over the fence. He studied the yard with jerky head movements.

'Can you see it?' cried a babyish voice. Di!

Bruiser shook his head. Suddenly Bruiser was looking straight at

Mitch's window. He wore a mean scowl.

Bet he thinks I took it, thought Mitch edging back from the window.

Understanding Narratives   Circle a letter to answer questions 1 to 8.

1. How can the reader tell that Mitch and Bruce were about the same age?
    A   they were enrolled in the same class
    B   they lived next door to each other
    C   they were to attend the same school
    D   they wanted to play together

2. What is the most likely reason Mitch had not met Bruce?
    A   Mitch didn't go out into his own backyard
    B   Mitch had just moved into the house next door
    C   Bruce was the bully at Mitch's school
    D   Bruce was not allowed to play with his neighbours

3. Mitch thought that going to the Bull place would be like
    A   working in a rockery   B   starting school in a new class
    C   going into an enemy camp   D   finding a new friend

4. What job did Mitch have to do for his mother?
    He had to
    A   be a watch-out from the bedroom window
    B   stack the removalist's cartons outside
    C   get himself ready for school
    D   help his mother unpack cartons

5. Mitch thought Bruce was very strong because Bruce
    A   could climb a fence   B   picked on kids to bully
    C   threw balls into backyards   D   could lift heavy rocks

6. Which word best describes the look on Bruce's face?
    A   scared   B   worried
    C   mean   D   upset

7. How did Mitch's mother feel when she returned from the Bull's house?
    A   pleased   B   bothered   C   nervous   D   amused

8. According to the text, which statement is CORRECT?
    A   Mitch's mother and Bruce's mother were long-time friends.
    B   Bruce first saw Mitch when he took cartons outside.
    C   It took two people to put rocks in the wheelbarrow.
    D   Di is the youngest person in the text.

Need to try another narrative? Check the contents page.

Lit Tip 24 – Improve your literacy skills   Alliteration

We have **alliteration** when the same letter or sound occurs at the beginning of words that are close together in the text: mighty mouse, clean clothes

In the text Meet Bruiser, Mitch refers to Bruce as Bruiser Bull the Boss. The alliteration is caused by the repetition of the B sound. Alliteration can add interest to your writing.

Underline the letters that are used for alliteration in these examples.

1. whispering wind   2. chubby little chickens   3. slip, slap slop

Write your own alliteration words for: funny _____

Understanding Year 4 Comprehension
A. Horsfield © Five Senses Education © W. Marlin

Summer Adventure

Characters: *Goldie, Len, Brian, Carol (all about the same age, dressed for the beach)*
Scene: *a bus stop shelter, with the children looking about in a bewildered way.*

Goldie:	Why are we at a bus stop? No one said anything about passing a bus stop.
Len:	Well, Uncle Joe said we wouldn't need a bus. It's walking distance.
Goldie:	Maybe we took a wrong turn. We should be able to hear the sea by now.
Brian:	And smell it.
Len:	We should have turned right at the second intersection.
Carol:	Dad said to turn left first then right!
Len:	We certainly don't need a bus. Not for a few hundred metres!
Brian:	We should start again. Retrace our steps - or something.
Goldie:	That would mean doing the turns back-to-front. We would have to turn left when we turned right, wouldn't we?
Len:	I'm getting confused - and hot. Let's keep going until we find the beach or a beach sign.
Brian:	If we are heading away from the beach there won't be a sign Stupid!

(Goldie sees a bus timetable on a bus shelter support pole. She has a closer look. She looks at her watch.)

Goldie:	There's a bus in...due now!
Brian:	We'll stop it and tell the driver to stop at the beach.
Len:	That's stupid! He can't take us to the beach if he's not going there!
Carol:	We can ask him - or her.
Brian:	Bus drivers are all men!
Len:	Anything is better than hanging around in this heat. All I want is a swim.
Carol:	Complaining is not helping anyone.
Len:	Here comes a bus! Wave it to stop!

(Goldie moves to the front of the stage and signals the bus to stop. They all follow the bus go past with their eyes.)

Len:	It went straight past! What do we do now?
Carol:	Did you see its sign? NOT IN SERVICE.

(Goldie has another look at the bus timetable.)

Goldie:	Oh no!
Brian and Len:	What?
Goldie:	I was looking at Sunday's timetable.

Today is Saturday!

(The children groan and look exhausted.)

Understanding Play Scripts   Circle a letter to answer questions 1 to 8.

1. The children are getting more and more upset with each other because
    A   Goldie is becoming bossy
    B   no one is interested in going to the beach
    C   tempers are beginning to flare out of frustration
    D   Uncle Joe had given them the wrong directions

2. The children arrived at a bus stop shelter because they
    A   were given the wrong directions   B   decided it was too hot to walk
    C   had taken a wrong turn   D   planned to catch a bus to the beach

3. Which person thinks all bus drivers are men?
    A   Goldie   B   Len   C   Carol   D   Brian

4. The bus displays a sign: NOT IN SERVICE.
    The sign NOT IN SERVICE means that the
    A   bus is not on a regular route   B   engine is causing problems
    C   driver is lost   D   destination of the bus in unknown

5. What mistake did Goldie make?
    A   the time the bus would arrive
    B   the distance of the walk to the beach
    C   the correct turns to make to get back home
    D   the day that the bus would stop at the bus stop

6. In the information, in the **Scene** (second line) you are told the children looked *'about in a bewildered way'*. This implies that the children were
    A   expecting to see the beach   B   confused about where they were
    C   worried they had missed the bus   D   getting hot from walking

7. How did the children feel when they found a bus stop
    A   surprised   B   desperate   C   relieved   D   excited

8. What would be a better title for this script?
    A   Waiting for the bus   B   Which way?
    C   Goldie finds a timetable   D   Not in service

Understanding Year 4 Comprehension
A. Horsfield © Five Senses Education © W. Marlin

Letter to the Editor

> Each week the Gillang Bay News prints a letter by a student in its Kids' Say section. This week's letter is by Donna James at Bayside State School.

Dear Editor,

Do you like to be woken up at 7 o'clock on Sunday mornings? I don't! And I'm sure not many other people do either.

Why do I ask this question? I will tell you. It seems that early on Sunday morning some people feel compelled to mow lawns - and some even use garden blowers. The noise is enough to wake me up.

But then I think about all those people who have had to work on Saturday night and I know how much they need a restful night. Shift workers, getting home from work need time during the day to get some sleep. Early morning mowing is unfair to these people. Sunday is supposed to be the day of rest.

Mowing at this time could be all right if people used electric mowers, but no, they all have those ones with petrol engines. Some of them actually roar as they do circuits of their yards. They are not well maintained. They are not only noisy but can create pollution as they chug filthy fumes into the clean morning air.

The noise doesn't stop there. The local dogs begin a barking <u>frenzy</u> at this disturbance. I feel like ringing the dog pound to take them away.

I make this request to the Sunday morning mowers. Please do your mowing on Saturday. If that's not possible, start later in the day. That shouldn't be too hard.

I hope you print my letter,

Donna James

(Good news Donna - we have published you (letter - editor)

Understanding Letters to the Editor Circle a letter or tick a box for questions 1 to 8.

1. What upsets Donna James the most
    - A   people using garden blowers
    - B   people who mow lawns on Sunday morning
    - C   fumes from petrol-driven lawn mowers
    - D   dogs that bark when she is trying to sleep

2. People who want to mow lawns early in the morning should
    - A   keep their dogs locked up
    - B   use a garden blower to clean up their lawn
    - C   use quieter electric mowers
    - D   write to the editor of the *Gillang Bay News*

3. Because of mower noise Donna feels most concern for
    - A   readers of *Gillang Bay News*   B   dog owners
    - C   people who mow on Saturdays   D   shift workers

4. Donna's letter could best be described as
    - A   a request for consideration   B   an unreasonable criticism
    - C   an amusing opinion   D   an angry reaction

5. The word *frenzy* in paragraph 5 means
    - A   annoyed by threats   B   sickened with a fever
    - C   frantic with distress   D   cheered by excitement

6. Who is Donna trying to persuade to change their ways with her letter?
    - A   Saturday workers   B   Sunday morning mowers
    - C   the newspaper editor   D   people who sleep in late

7. Did Donna get her letter to the paper editor printed?
    Tick a box.

    YES ☐   NO ☐

8. From Donna's letter, which of the following statements is an opinion and not a fact?
    - A   Sunday morning mowing starts the neighbourhood dogs barking.
    - B   Petrol mowers can pollute the air with fumes.
    - C   Shift workers need time during the day to get some sleep.
    - D   Sunday is supposed to be the day of rest.

Lit Tip 26 – Improve your literacy skills   Rhetorical questions

When we ask a question we usually expect an answer. There are situations where you don't really expect an answer. These questions are called rhetorical questions.

Has someone ever said to you: "Who do you think you are?" They don't expect you to answer this question. They are drawing your attention to something you are doing.

Donna James opens her letter with a rhetorical question. She doesn't expect an answer. She is trying to get the readers' interest and make them feel involved. This is a clever technique to use in your writing but don't use it too often.

Underline another rhetorical question in Donna's letter.

Understanding Year 4 Comprehension
A. Horsfield © Five Senses Education © W. Marlin

Headphones

Headphones may be as dangerous as jet engines. Turning the volume up too high on your headphones can damage the coating of the nerve cells of the ear, leading to temporary hearing loss according to university scientists.

When using headphones, personal music players can subject listeners to noise levels similar to those of jet engines. High noise levels are known to cause hearing problems such as temporary hearing loss and tinnitus. Tinnitus is the name given to a ringing or buzzing in the ears. It may be like the sound of distant waves on the shore or high-pitched buzzing. Only the person with the condition can hear it.

Nerve cells that carry electrical signals from the ear to the brain have a coating called the myelin sheath, which helps the electrical signals travel along the cell. Exposure to loud noises can strip the cells of this coating, disrupting the electrical signals. This means the nerves can no longer efficiently transmit information from the ear to the brain.

Sometimes the coating surrounding the nerve cells can reform, letting the cells function as normal again. This means hearing loss may be temporary and full hearing might be restored. However prolonged exposure to very loud noise may cause permanent damage. Headphones must be used with care.

Adapted from Tinnitus Talk March 2013 pp7, 8

Understanding Explanations   Circle a letter to answer questions 1 to 8.

1. According to the text how does loud noise affect a person's ears?
    A   it gives the person a headache
    B   it makes the person permanently deaf
    C   it causes the nerve coating to become thicker
    D   it damages the coating of the ear's nerve cells

2. Who found that turning up headphones to very loud can cause hearing loss?
    A   pilots of jet planes   B   university scientists
    C   manufacturers of headphones   D   headphone owners

3. What do nerve cells carry from the ear to the brain?
    A   a nerve coating   B   ear wax
    C   electrical signals   D   loud noise

4. The writer writes about *prolonged exposure* in paragraph 4.
    Prolonged exposure is exposure that
    A   lasts for longer than expected   B   is louder than most noises
    C   happens very often   D   is very difficult to tolerate

5. What advice is given to users of headphones?
    A   keep the loudness of music to the level of jet engine noise
    B   always use headphones with care to protect the ears
    C   never wear headphones to listen to music from a musical player
    D   any hearing loss caused by headphones can be repaired

6. According to the text, what can strip the nerve cells of their protective coating?
    A   the myelin sheaf   B   electrical signals
    C   loud noises   D   buzzing in the ears

7. *Tinnitus* refers to a condition of the
    A   ears   B   headphones   C   nerves   D   brain

8. This information would be useful for people who
    A   have permanent hearing loss   B   fly aeroplanes
    C   sell headphones   D   use music players a lot

Need to try another explanation? Check the contents page.

Understanding Year 4 Comprehension
A. Horsfield © Five Senses Education © W. Marlin

Parts of a Knife

A knife does not contain many parts. Beginning at the end that you hold closest to you is the butt. Rivets and scales hold the butt, or handle, to the tang. The tang is the piece of metal that flows through the end part of the knife. The bolster area connects the tang to the base of the knife. Next is the heel, which is the widest part of the knife. The 'unsharp' top is the spine. The edge is the sharp section that you cut with followed by the tip or point.

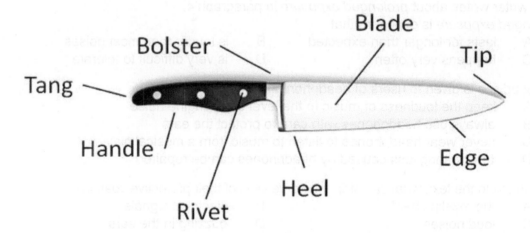

A knife is a tool that uses a blade to cut through solid matter. As force is applied, it is spread out along the blade, forcing the object being cut to separate. This is a better use of energy than simply pulling the same object apart.

The key element of a knife is its blade. Blades can be either plain or serrated. Serration adds saw teeth to the blade, making the cutting of certain matter easier. Serrated blades do not requiring much sharpening. The side of the blade used for cutting is called the edge and some knives have double edges. Double-edged knives are not used with meals.

If the blade is single-bladed and thicker on the back, this thicker part is called the spine. Spines often have a groove to lighten the overall blade weight. The thick part of the blade where it is joined to the butt, or handle, is called a ricasso - the short flat area directly in front of the handle.

Knife handles are made from a variety of materials including plastic and wood. Often dining knives have the handle and blade made from the same piece of metal.

Sources: http//www.ask.com/question/part-of-a-knife
      http://www.ehow.com/about_4673208_parts-knife.html

Understanding Reports   Circle a letter to answer questions 1 to 8.

1. What is the important part of a knife
   A handle   B blade   C heel   D tip

2. With a single-bladed knife what is the name of the part opposite the cutting edge of the blade?
   A spine   B ricasso   C tip   D blade

3. Looking at the diagram, the widest part of the knife is at the
   A handle   B rivet   C heel   D tang

4. What would be a good reason for knives used with meals to be single-bladed?
   A It would reduce their weight.   B They do not need to be sharpened.
   C It would save time cutting food.   D They would be safer to use.

5. Why is *unsharp* ('unsharp') in inverted commas?
   A it stresses the fact that it is **not** the sharp edge
   B there is no opposite word for *sharp*
   C *unsharp* has been spelled incorrectly
   D the writer knows it is not a real word

6. The bolster section of a knife
   A is the sharpest edge of the blade
   B provides protection for the knife user
   C connects the tang to the base of the knife
   D separates the handle from the point

7. What is meant by the word *key* as used in paragraph 3 of the text?
   A a piece of metal used to open a lock
   B the most important part of an implement
   C any sharpened piece of metal
   D the solution to a problem

8. What can be used to hold the knife handle to the tang?
   A heel   B bolster   C rivets   D point

Lit Tip 28 – Improve your literacy skills   What are puns?

A **pun** is a humorous play on words to emphasise two different meanings or uses of words that are alike or sound alike. If you want to write amusing stories puns can add to the humour.

Pun example: A book called *The rat's tale*. The word tale is used as a pun because it could mean the rat's actual tail or a story (tale) about a rat

Can you spot the puns in these?

A boiled egg is hard to beat for breakfast.

Two silk worms had a race. They ended up in a tie!

I used to be a calm doctor but I just lost my patients.

Seven days without food makes one weak.

Being struck by lightning is a shocking experience.

A horse is a very stable animal.

Fish are smart – they live in schools!

Did you know? Shakespeare used puns in many of his plays – over 500 years ago!

Home Page

HOME	MAP	HISTORY	CLIMATE	ACTIVITIES	CONTACTS

You are here.

Discover the real WEST of Western Australia

Norseman, "the Eastern gate to the Western Australia", is a major stopping point for travellers to and from the Eastern States and is an ideal place to take a refreshing break in your journey after crossing the Nullarbor Plain.

Photo: A. Horsfield

Camel trains were an early form of transport to Norseman

Norseman is situated 726 km east of Perth and 717 km from the WA - SA border on the Eyre Hwy.

Find us on Facebook!

Norseman Fact
Norseman is <u>unique</u>. It is the only town in Australia named after a horse!
In 1894 gold put Norseman on the map when the prospector, Laurie Sinclair, dropped in on his brother on his way to Esperance. He tethered his horse, "Hardy Norseman", overnight and in the morning was amazed to discover that it had pawed up a gold nugget. A rich gold reef was discovered and thousands flocked to the area make their fortune.

As well as gold -
there are many other minerals and gemstones in the region. It is possible to fossick for agates in a peaceful bushland setting just short way from the town.
Permits required.

Between Norseman and the WA border drivers come across this sign on the Eyre Hwy. How many people have driven this length of road?

Photo: A. Horsfield

90 MILE STRAIGHT
AUSTRALIA'S LONGEST STRAIGHT ROAD
145.6 km

Click here for:
Community Markets   Norseman Rocks   Tin Camels
Eyre Hwy Tourism Office   Hardy Norseman statue

Hardy Norseman photo from:
http://www.virtualtourist.com/travel/Australia_and_Oceania/Australia/State_of_Western_Australia/
Norseman-1871829/Things_To_Do-Norseman-TG-C-1.html#page=1&tgCount=0&themes=82

Understanding Web Pages   Circle a letter or write an answer for questions 1 to 8.

1. A good word to describe the location of Norseman would be:
    A   new   B   remote   C   wet   D   modern

2. Why were camels brought to Norseman?
    A   to help look for gold
    B   to model for tin statues in town
    C   to carry people across the Nullarbor Plain
    D   to bring goods in for the early settlers

3. What does the word *unique* mean?
    A   the only one of its kind   B   unusual
    C   outstanding   D   isolated

4. Where can agate be found in the Norseman region?
    A   on the Nullabor plain   B   on the SA - WA border
    C   in bushland near Norseman   D   along the 90 Mile Straight

5. If I wanted to find out about the weather in Norseman I should CLICK on the tab for
    A   MAP   B   HISTORY   C   CLIMATE   D   ACTIVITIES

6. The people at Norseman would like inter-state road travellers to
    A   ride a Norseman camel   B   take a short break in Norseman
    C   visit Laurie Sinclair's brother   D   cross the Nullarbor Plain

7. How many <u>kilometres</u> long is the road called *90 Mile Straight*?

    Write your answer in the box. ☐ kilometres

8. According to the HOME PAGE what would be an interesting activity for visitors staying in Norseman?
    A   look for the Hardy Norseman statue
    B   set up a stall in the community markets
    C   walk the length of the Eyre Highway
    D   search for gemstones in nearby bushland

Lit Tip 29 – Improve your literacy skills   *un* and *im* for antonyms

Remember: Antonyms are words with opposite meanings: good/bad
For many adjectives the opposite can be made by adding the prefix *un* or *im*.
For most words the prefix *un* makes the antonym (opposite).
Examples include: happy/unhappy, done/undone, aware/unaware, sure/unsure.
For a number of words that start with p or m we use the prefix im.
Examples include: pure/impure, perfect/imperfect, polite/impolite, mobile/immobile
Using a prefix write the opposites of these words.

proper _____ , able _____ , fed _____ , true _____ ,

known _____ , patient _____ , mature _____ , read _____ .

Understanding Year 4 Comprehension
A. Horsfield © Five Senses Education © W. Marlin

Be Glad Your Nose is on Your Face

Be glad your nose is on your face,
not pasted on some other place,
for if it were where it is not,
you might dislike your nose a lot.

Imagine if your precious nose
were <u>sandwiched in between your toes</u>,
that clearly would not be a treat,
for you'd be forced to smell your feet.

Your nose would be a source of <u>dread</u>
were it attached atop your head,
it soon would drive you to despair,
forever tickled by your hair.

Within your ear, your nose would be
an absolute catastrophe,
for when you were obliged to sneeze,
your brain would rattle from the breeze.

Your nose, instead, through thick and thin,
remains between your eyes and chin,
not pasted on some other place-
be glad your nose is on your face!

Jack Prelutsky (1940 -)

From: http://www.poemhunter.com/jack-prelutsky/

Understanding Poetry   Circle a letter or write an answer for questions 1 to 8.

1. This poem by Jack Prelutsky is intended to
    A   amuse the reader   B   warn the reader of dangers
    C   upset the reader   D   frighten the reader

2. If your nose were on the top of your head
    A   your brain would rattle when you sneezed
    B   you would smell many unpleasant things
    C   it would get tickled by your hair
    D   you would have to wear a hat

3. The word *dread* as used in stanza 3 has similar meaning to
    A   dead   B   worry   C   wonder   D   fear

4. The writer has used the words: *sandwiched in between your toes*.
    By this he means
    A   having food between your toes
    B   squeezed between two of your toes
    C   having toes that taste like sandwiches
    D   it's time to care for your feet

5. What word does the poet use to rhyme with nose?

    Write your answer in the box. ☐

6. If your nose were between your toes you would have to smell
    A   the footpath   B   your feet
    C   your shoes or socks   D   things on the ground

7. If your nose were in your ear you should be careful not to
    A   sneeze   B   inhale   C   breathe   D   smell

8. The poet suggests the best place for a nose is
    A   on top of your head   B   on your feet
    C   in your ear   D   between your eyes and chin

Lit Tip 30 – Improve your literacy skills   Repetition

When we write stories using the same word too often it make the story boring. We must be careful not to overuse such words as then, and he/she, and I. Repetition of these words (and some others) doesn't improve the story.

However, some writers use repetition to improve their stories. Look at these examples.

That day was very, very hot! By repeating very the writer is stressing how hot it was!

It was a long, long way home. This means it was a very long way home.

The rain came down, pitter-patter, pitter-patter. It rained a lot!

Ben's eyes were black, his hair was black and his thoughts were black! What kind of boy do you think Ben was?

Read Meet Bruiser (text 24) again.

What word has the author repeated when Bruiser loads the wheelbarrow?

Write your answer here. _____

Remember to use repetition to improve your story writing but don't use it too often!

Understanding Year 4 Comprehension
A. Horsfield © Five Senses Education © W. Marlin

The Mary Celeste Mystery

The most famous unsolved mystery of the oceans involves the sailing ship, Mary Celeste.

On a fine day in December 1872 a sailor on the Dei Gratia spied the Mary Celeste sailing an erratic course in the Atlantic Ocean about 100km out from Europe. It appeared to be in trouble. The Dei Gratia captain decided to investigate and sailed towards the Mary Celeste.

As he neared the ship he noticed something strange – there was no one at the wheel or on the deck. The Dei Gratia's crew called to the ship but there was no reply.

Three men from the Dei Gratia boarded then searched the Mary Celeste. There was no one on board, but some of the ship's equipment was scattered around. The crew's personal belongings were still in place, including valuables. There was plenty of food and water. The cargo of hundreds of barrels of alcohol was almost untouched except for a few that were empty or damaged.

The last <u>entry</u> in the ship's log was for early November. The ship's compass and lifeboats were missing. None of those on board were ever seen or heard from again.

Dei Gratia's crew sailed the boat to Gibraltar (near Spain).

Ten people were on board the Mary Celeste when it left New York for Italy in November. No trace has ever been found of them and the mystery has never been solved.

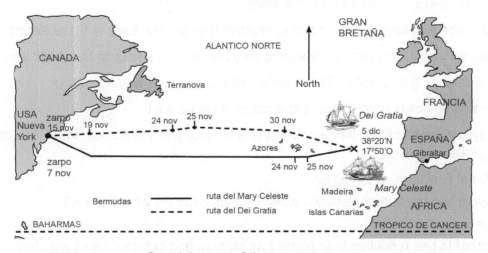

Spanish map of the voyage

Understanding Recounts   Circle a letter or write an answer for questions 1 to 8.

1. What first alerted the crew of Dei Gratia that something was amiss with the Mary Celeste?
   - A   no one answered the calls from the Dei Gratia
   - B   the ship appeared to have no set course
   - C   the Dei Gratia's crew could not see anyone on board the Mary Celeste
   - D   the Mary Celeste was in the middle of the Atlantic Ocean

2. The text suggests the Mary Celeste had been drifting crewless for
   - A   a few days
   - B   a week
   - C   several weeks
   - D   about a year

3. How many people were on the Mary Celeste when it left New York?
   - A   0
   - B   3
   - C   7
   - D   10

4. What puzzles people about the Mary Celeste mystery?
   - A   some of the ship's equipment was scattered around
   - B   its food and water supply had not run out
   - C   why the Dei Gratia's crew sailed the ship to Gibraltar
   - D   there was no apparent reason to abandon ship

5. Write the numbers 1 to 4 in the boxes to show the correct order in which events occurred in the report. The first one (1) has been done for you.

1	The Mary Celeste was observed sailing erratically.
	Crew from the Dei Gratia sailed the Mary Celeste to Gibraltar.
	The Mary Celeste was boarded by crew from the Dei Gratia.
	Crew from the Dei Gratia found broken barrels of alcohol.

6. What did the crew find had been damaged on the Mary Celeste?
   - A   lifeboats
   - B   the ship's wheel
   - C   barrels of alcohol
   - D   the ship's equipment

7. What part of speech is the word *entry* as used in paragraph 5?
   - A   noun
   - B   preposition
   - C   verb
   - D   adjective

8. Look at the map. In which direction was the Mary Celeste's planned course?
   - A   north
   - B   south
   - C   east
   - D   west

Lit Tip 31 – Improve your literacy skills   What are homonyms?

Homonyms are two or more words that have the same spelling but different meanings.

The word ring can be used in several ways.

It is a noun in these sentences.   Mum wears a wedding ring.

The clown hopped into the circus ring.

It is a verb in this sentence.   Dad will ring Grandpa on his birthday.

Can you see the different meanings for card(nouns) in these sentences.

My card is an ace of hearts.   Jeff lost his credit card in the shopping mall.

Write the part of speech for the homonyms in these sentences.

1. A fly was on the food! [   ]   The pilot can fly a jumbo jet. [   ]

2. 2 Did the coach address the team? [   ]   My address is in Ryde. [   ]

Understanding Year 4 Comprehension
A. Horsfield © Five Senses Education © W. Marlin

Strange Meeting

I had just left Swan St and was in Pegasus Lane when I heard the noisiest squabble ever coming from the community hall. It sounded like a disturbed flock of galahs.

'Messy Pig!'   'Grub!'   'Old Hen!'

'Cuckoo!' Then a burst of hysterical laughter. I stopped dead in my tracks.

'Ratbag!' More screams of laughter. This was no ordinary argument.

What was going on? Someone suddenly knocked on a table. Knock! Knock! Knock! Then calm.

A meeting, I guessed, as I spied a notice taped to a window.

> **AIM Headquarters**
> **(Animal Insult Makers)**
> Meets here secretly - first Thursday each month.
> Don't be a daffy duck - join the crusade.
> All Welcome

What did AIM do, I wondered. They certainly had fun – strange fun, but fun all the same. But why were they secretive?

A boy suddenly walked up the front steps and rang the doorbell that sounded like an angry sheep, then waited.

Behind the slowly opening door a suspicious face peeked out. Soft words were shared. I heard "jackass" loudly whispered followed by a burst of laughter. The boy was <u>ushered</u> inside with a wide welcoming smile.

I was startled by an unexpected movement. Suddenly someone was standing by my elbow. She had appeared, whoosh! out of nowhere. One moment nothing, then Bingo! Beside me was this girl, wearing a bright blue costume with a short red cape. She was scowling at the hall. She looked like some sort of ____(6)____.

'They're at it again,' she muttered angrily.

Taken aback, I said the first thing that came into my head. 'They're certainly enjoying themselves, even if their language is … unusual.'

'Unusual? Maybe. And at whose expense?' she snapped, her chin jutting.

Bursts of excited shouts drowned my reply. 'Slimy snake!' 'Dumb ox!' 'Batty!'

Understanding Narratives   Circle a letter to answer questions 1 to 8.

1. The narrator discovered a secret meeting being held
    A   in Swan St   B   on the steps of a community hall
    C   near a private zoo   D   in a Pegasus Lane hall

2. What were the people at the meeting doing?
    A   making fun of animal names   B   taking care of upset pets
    C   planning to go to a farm   D   having a noisy argument

3. The narrative is recorded in
    A   first person   B   second person   C   third person

4. How did the girl in the bright blue costume react to the behaviour at the meeting?
    A   She laughed hysterically.   B   She expressed her annoyance.
    C   She was fascinated.   D   She was taken by surprise.

5. Which of these lines is an example of a simile?
    A   Someone suddenly knocked on a table.
    B   One moment nothing, then Bingo!
    C   It sounded like a disturbed flock of galahs.
    D   I stopped dead in my tracks.

6. A word has been removed from the text at (6).
    What would be a suitable word for that space?
    A   princess   B   superhero   C   policewoman   D   film star

7. The word *ushered* infers that the visiting boy
    A   had changed his mind   B   paid to join the meeting
    C   was very important   D   was guided inside

8. Someone in the hall knocked three times on a table.
    This suggests that someone was
    A   trying to get some quiet to start a meeting
    B   involved in an argument that was becoming violent
    C   warning members of a visitor at the front door
    D   wanting to create as much noise as possible

Need to try another narrative? Check the contents page.

Lit Tip 32 – Improve your literacy skills   Initials or Acronyms

Many companies and government departments are known by their initials or by an acronym. What is the difference? **Initials** don't make words. For example for South Australia we say S then A. We don't say SA (to rhyme with pa).

Acronyms are words made from initials. For QANTAS and ANZAC we say the words not the separate letters.

Common nouns can be formed from acronyms such as laser and scuba, but important people and places have capital letters. There are no stops between the capital letters.

Tick the box if the initials make an acronym.

NASA ☐   DVD ☐   NAPLAN ☐   PM ☐   QLD ☐   ABC ☐   TEN ☐   radar ☐

Understanding Year 4 Comprehension
A. Horsfield © Five Senses Education © W. Marlin

How Fog Lights Work

Fog lights are designed to reduce glare that occurs while driving a vehicle through thick fog. On a foggy road, most of the light is reflected from the water droplets in the fog back to the driver. The droplets work like a mirror. When headlights are switched on in a fog, most of the light is thrown back into the driver's eyes creating a blinding patch of light.

Angling for Better Vision

Fog lights are meant to reduce the amount of glare thrown back. The lights are angled downward toward the road, so when they are turned on, the light is thrown across the road in front of the car and not straight ahead, where it can be reflected back into the driver's eyes. This gives some visibility of the roadway, without the blinding effect.

Benefits and *Drawbacks*

Fog lights will give a little more visibility and reduce glare while driving down a foggy road. Drivers will be able to see the roadway more clearly and suffer less glare.

The trouble is that fog lights only light up a small section of road, because they are angled and mounted lower on the vehicle. They may not give drivers enough warning of obstacles. They do not cut through the fog as the lights themselves use the same bulbs as the headlights.

The colour of the lights has no bearing on their use in fog. Yellow or any other colour is not recognized as being "better" at penetrating fog. Yellow lights may reduce some of the blinding glare, which makes them appear to cut through the fog. They may be useful as a warning to on coming traffic.

Source: http://www.ehow.com/how-does_4885332_fog-lights-work.html

Understanding Explanations
Circle a letter or write an answer for questions 1 to 8.

1. Where are fog lights placed on a car?
    - A   next to the headlights
    - B   between the headlights
    - C   close to the road
    - D   above other lights

2. According to the text fog lights on cars use the same bulbs as in the headlights.
    Is this statement TRUE or FALSE? Tick a box.

    TRUE ☐   FALSE ☐

3. Fog lights work well because they
    - A   reduce glare for the driver
    - B   are brighter and stronger
    - C   are coloured to penetrate fog
    - D   light up larger lengths of road

4. The light from fog lights is directed
    - A   above the light from the headlights
    - B   down onto the road
    - C   into the oncoming traffic
    - D   to either side of the vehicle

5. One of the problems with fog lights is that they
    - A   confuse oncoming drivers
    - B   cannot be distinguished from other lights
    - C   are weaker than headlights
    - D   may not reveal obstacles soon enough

6. When headlights shine into fog the fog acts like a
    - A   wall
    - B   mirror
    - C   pond
    - D   glass

7. Which word from the text has the opposite meaning of **Benefits**?

    Write your answer on the line. _____

8. It would be important to have this information available at a
    - A   learn-to-drive school
    - B   motor repair garage
    - C   new car showroom
    - D   public transport office

Need to try another explanation? Check the contents page.

Lit Tip 33 – Improve your literacy skills   **Punctuation in speech**

It is often difficult to know where to put the punctuation marks when writing speech in your stories.

The full stop goes inside the inverted commas.

Look at this sentence: **Jack said, "I am ready to go."**

A comma comes after said to indicate a pause.

The question mark goes inside the inverted commas.

Try this one: **Jill asked, "Who are you?"**

A comma comes after said-type words to indicate a pause.

Punctuate this sentence: **Dad called   Can you see the bin**

Understanding Year 4 Comprehension
A. Horsfield © Five Senses Education © W. Marlin

Gillang Bay at Night

There was a ship anchored in Gillang Bay, its masts tall and bare against the rising moon. There was little breeze. The gently rippling water reflected the moon and stars as shimmering sources of light that formed strange patterns with the slowly bobbing reflection of the yellow light from the ship's cabin. Someone must be on board.

Along the nearby mudflats were hunters for mud crabs. Some were carrying lanterns while others had torches. The torchlights would dart madly about across the black expanse before disappearing for a few moments. The lantern lights were calmer. They moved in warm glows steadily on before changing course or even settling in the one spot as if having a rest. Of course, they weren't. Most likely the crab hunters had made a find and had put the lantern down on a firmer mound of mud, while they made sure of a capture. The unlucky crab, no doubt, ending up in a bag with some of its neighbours.

Unseen and in the distance a small outboard buzzed through the dimness, like some agitated insect angry at being disturbed by the <u>night prowlers</u> along the shallows.

On the shadowed headland to the harbour the lighthouse light was more insistent. It blinked every few seconds like a faulty neon light. But it was working as it should, boldly warning those sailing the water of its presence and to take care.

Understanding Descriptions Circle a letter or write an answer for questions 1 to 8.

1. Why did the writer suspect there was someone on the ship?
   - A he heard people on board
   - B it was about to leave the bay
   - C the ship was at anchor
   - D a light was on in a cabin

2. Name one item the hunters of mud crabs carried?

   Write your answer on the line, _____

3. What sound did the writer hear on the bay?
   - A the lighthouse workers
   - B the mud crab hunters
   - C an outboard motor
   - D someone on the sailing boat

4. Which of the following is a simile from the text?
   - A its masts tall and bare against the rising moon
   - B boldly warning the world of its presence and to take care
   - C a small outboard buzzed through the dimness
   - D like some agitated insect angry at being disturbed

5. What is the most likely reason the writer refers to the mud crabs as *unlucky*?
   - A the crabs could suffocate in the bag
   - B the crabs would end up being cooked
   - C the crabs would be released somewhere new
   - D the crabs could die out of water

6. Ships near Gillang Bay were being warned to take care by
   - A people on the anchored sailing ship
   - B men on the mudflats with torches
   - C the blinking lighthouse light
   - D the driver of the boat with the outboard motor

7. Which word best describes the Gillang Bay scene?
   - A peaceful   B sinister   C cheerful   D alarming

8. In paragraph 4 the writer talks of *night prowlers*?
   The *night prowlers are*
   - A people in motorboats
   - B hunters of mud crabs
   - C crew from the sailing ship
   - D lighthouse operators

Lit Tip 34 – Improve your literacy skills   What is an idiom?

Idiom refers to a group of words that has a meaning that is not obvious from the literal meaning of the words. We all use idioms and usually know what they mean.

An example would be the best way to explain idiom. When we say, "I didn't come down in the last shower," we are not talking about the rain. We are actually saying, "I'm not stupid. Don't try to fool me with your ideas."

Don't spit the dummy means don't lose your temper. Nothing to do with dummies!

Can you explain the meaning behind this idiom?

If you are told you are up a gum tree it means you are _____

Understanding Year 4 Comprehension
A. Horsfield © Five Senses Education © W. Marlin

Making a Potato Print

A creative way to make a print is to use a potato!

Potato printing is fairly simple and the most difficult part is getting the hang of cutting into the potato. You will need an adult to help with this part. The cutting is definitely not recommended for young children.

Although potatoes are great food, they are fine for making a potato print. Materials that are needed for potato printing are: clean potatoes, paper, a sharp knife, tempera paint and a brush.

The first step is to cut the potato in half and start with simple shapes, such as a square, a diamond or circle. When you get a little more skill you can make letters of the alphabet. Remember, you will need to draw the letter backwards so that it will print the correct way.

Once you decide on a shape for your print, draw the shape on the flat side of one of the halves of the potatoes. Cut away the potato that is around your design.

The next step is to spread paint on the flat edge of the raised design.

Press the painted shape against flat paper to make a potato print. Repeat this as many times as you wish and as long as the potato holds up. Change colours to get different coloured shapes.

A different method to carving the potato is made by removing all the potato from within the design - a sunken shape. When you print you have the round potato shape with a white inner shape.

As you become more experienced with potato carving, your designs will become more complex, making more interesting potato prints.

Source: http://voices.yahoo.com/how-potato-print-2186486.html?cat=7

Understanding Procedures Circle a letter or write an answer for questions 1 to 8.

1. Making potato prints would be a suitable activity for
   - A children in pre-school art classes
   - B parents keen to keep children occupied
   - C full time pattern makers
   - D professional house painters

2. After you have collected the items you need to make a potato print, what is the first step?
   - A paint the potato
   - B choose a letter for your design
   - C cut the potato in half
   - C select a shape for a print

3. It is advised that a young child attempting potato printing should
   - A use a sharp knife
   - B get the help of an adult
   - C wait until they get older
   - D have a supply of potatoes

4. What is the brush required for?
   - A add paint to the part of the potato to be printed
   - B remove dirt from the potato
   - C paint the paper before the print is made
   - D paint around the shape made by the potato print

5. Making a potato print could best be described as a
   - A complicated series of steps
   - B very dangerous craft activity
   - C cooking experiment
   - D simple way to occupy young children

6. Write the numbers 1 to 4 in the boxes to show the correct order in which events should occur in this procedure. The first one (1) has been done for you.

	remove the potato flesh from around the shape you have drawn
1	cut the potato in half
	draw a shape on the potato surface
	paint the raised shape with tempera paint

7. How many prints can be made with each potato design?
   - A one
   - B a few
   - C about five
   - D many

8. According to the text which statement is CORRECT?
   - A The potato should be painted before it is carved.
   - B The only letter that can be made with a potato print is H.
   - C Two different prints can be made from one potato.
   - D The potato should be cooked before used to make a potato print.

Need to try another procedure? Check the contents page.

Puppy Academy Training School

Charlie found this flier in her parents' letterbox.

Puppy Academy Training School (PATS)
Puppy Academy Training School (PATS) is the most important step you can take to give the newest family friend a great start in its canine life.

Enrol your puppy in for any of our training courses and you will be thrilled with the results - could be an A in every course!
You will be as happy as a puppy - and so will your new companion!

Puppy Kinder
(8 - 18 weeks of age)
At PATS we cover a range of puppy **behaviours** for all puppy types.

☑ Chewing ☑ Scratching
☑ Digging ☑ Jumping
☑ Biting
   and, of course -
☑ Toilet training!

At PATS we teach your puppy to **socialise** with:

☑ children and toddlers
☑ other people
☑ other puppies
☑ strange noises

We **teach** your puppy to
☑ respond to a leash
☑ follow commands
   (Sit, Heel, Stay, Come, Drop)
☑ respond to a whistle

Classes are held every morning at 9 a.m. except for Mondays.

Pooch Primary Classes
(4 - 7 months of age)
Primary classes are the best way to get the most fun from your young dog.
PATS cover a range of puppy **behaviours**:

☑ Toilet training
☑ Jumping, digging, biting
☑ Unnecessary barking

PATS teaches your puppy to **socialise** with:

☑ children
☑ other people
☑ other puppies
☑ unfamiliar places

We **teach** your puppy to
☑ respond to a leash
☑ follow commands
   (Sit, Heel, Stay, Come, Drop)
☑ respond to calls

Classes are held every morning at 11 a.m. except for Mondays.

NOTE: All puppies must be: • booked in before lessons start
• vaccinated

Understanding Persuasion Circle a letter or tick a box for questions 1 to 8.

1. Before a pup can be accepted into obedience classes it must
   - A   be able to respond to calls
   - B   have been vaccinated
   - C   be less than 8 weeks old
   - D   hear a whistle

2. When could a 4-month old pup have a training lesson?
   - A   9 a.m. on Mondays
   - B   11 a.m. on Mondays
   - C   9 a.m. on any day except Monday
   - D   11 a.m. on any day except Monday

3. The word PATS as used in the flier is an acronym.
   Tick a box for TRUE or FALSE.

   TRUE ☐   FALSE ☐

4. The staff at PATS are mainly concerned with
   - A   helping owners enjoy their pet dogs
   - B   getting owners to vaccinate their dogs
   - C   ensuring all dogs are kept on a leash
   - D   keeping dogs safe when away from home

5. What is treated in **Pooch Primary Classes** that is **not** treated in **Puppy Kinder?**
   - A   dog toilet training
   - B   control of unnecessary barking
   - C   how to react to other dogs
   - D   how to follow commands

6. Which word is used in the flier refers to dogs of all ages and breeds?
   - A   friend   B   academy   C   canine   D   puppy

7. The word *socialise*, as used in the flier means to
   - A   be well behaved in an acceptable way
   - B   enjoy life with other dogs
   - C   have many doggie friends
   - D   ignore things that can be distractions

8. At PATS they treat dogs as
   - A   wild animals that must be taught to obey
   - B   unwelcome visitors in their school
   - C   naughty puppies that are difficult to socialise
   - D   new members of their families

Need to try another persuasion? Check the contents page.

Lit Tip 36 – Improve your literacy skills   Dual ownership

An apostrophe s ('s) is used to show someone owns something, e.g. Bert's hair.

What do you do if two people own the same thing? What if Dan and Ned own a truck?

We write (and say): Dan and Ned's truck. The 's only goes on the last person's name.

Two more examples: the king and queen's castle   OR   the dog and cat's food

Rewrite this sentence correctly: Dad's and Mum's invitation was lost.

Understanding Year 4 Comprehension
A. Horsfield © Five Senses Education © W. Marlin

Young Don Bradman

Sir Donald Bradman (1908–2001) was born in the small town of Cootamundra, NSW. He was often called 'The Don'. He was considered to be the greatest Australian cricketer of all time. Sir Donald Bradman played serious cricket in his childhood and his teens.

During that time, cricket was just another game for Sir Donald – hitting golf balls with a cricket stump against a tank was his favourite pastime! This activity helped him to improve his reflexes and coordinate his hand movements with his eyesight.

Slowly he played more cricket with local clubs and his school. He scored centuries with amazing regularity. His first century when he was 12 years old, was scored when playing at Bowral Public School against Mittagong High School.

In 1920, Don saw his first test match at the Sydney Cricket Ground. When cricketer Charlie McCartney scored 170 runs he told his father that his ambition was to play at the Sydney Cricket ground! Later, he was invited to practice at this ground!

During the home series in 1932 against England, Sir Don scored 468 runs during his eight innings with two centuries and two half centuries. He went on to become one of the greatest Test Batsmen, with an incredible batting average of 99.94.

Later in 1932 Sir Don was the Australian team's captain. When the Australian team went to England for a test series, Sir Don was able to score 974 runs in 8 innings and came back to Australia as a great hero! Sir Donald died when he was 92 years old. Sir Don will never _____(8)_____.

Bradman was knighted in 1949 – Sir Donald Bradman – for his services to cricket.

In 1997 a postage stamp was issued in his honour. In 2008 on the centenary of his birth, the Royal Australian Mint issued a $5 gold coin with Bradman's image.

Source: http://www.streetdirectory.com/travel_guide/42259/recreation_and_sports/life_of_sir_donald_bradman.html

Understanding Recounts Circle a letter or write an answer for questions 1 to 8.

1. Sir Donald Bradman developed his eye-ball skills by
   A   hitting golf balls against tank with a cricket stump
   B   playing cricket in school and club teams
   C   watching cricket with his father at the Sydney Cricket Ground
   D   practicing cricket at the Sydney Cricket Ground

2. When did Sir Donald declare that he really wanted to play test cricket?
   A   while playing for Bowral Public School against Mittagong High School
   B   when he saw cricketer Charlie McCartney score 170 runs
   C   while he was playing club cricket in his home town
   D   when his batting average reached 99.94

3. The Sir Donald Bradman $5 gold coin was issued after Bradman's death.
   Is this statement TRUE or FALSE?
   Tick a box.   TRUE   [ ]   FALSE   [ ]

4. Where did Donald Bradman score his first century?
   A   Cootamundra (NSW)   B   Bowral Public School
   C   Sydney Cricket Ground   D   England

5. Which event most influenced Donald Bradman to take up a cricketing career?
   A   playing cricket for his school   B   joining the local cricket club
   C   becoming the Australian captain   D   Charlie McCartney scoring 170 runs

6. Write the numbers 1 to 4 in the boxes to show the correct order in which events occurred in the text. The first one (1) has been done for you.

[ ]	Don Bradman scored 468 runs during his eight innings against England.
[ ]	Don Bradman's services to cricket portrayed on a postage stamp.
[ ]	Don Bradman captains the Australian team to play England.
[1]	Don Bradman scores his first century.

7. In which year was Bradman awarded the title Sir?
   A   1920   B   1939   C   1949   D   1997

8. Some words have been left off paragraph 6 at (8). Which words would best complete this paragraph?
   A   play at the Sydney Cricket Ground again.
   B   be forgotten by cricketers, fans or by the Australians.
   C   return to England to play another test match.
   D   get another award or commendation for his cricket.

Lit Tip 37 – Improve your literacy skills   Writing the date

In Australia the order in writing the date is day, month, year, e.g. 22 January 1939.

There are no commas with this method. The century need not be included; 39 for 1939

You will also note that there is **no** nd after 22. We don't include the ordinal abbreviations (first/st, second/nd, third/rd and so on).

Write your birth date here. _____

If the day of the week is included a comma is used: Monday, 22 January 1939.

You may write the date with four numerals only: 22/01/39 or 22.01.39

If you talk about decades you may say the nineteen-eighties. This would be written as 1980s. There is **no** apostrophe s ('s) after 1980.

First Day at School

A million-billion-willion miles from home
Waiting for the bell to go. (To go where?)
Why are they all so big, other children?
So noisy? So much at home they
Must have been born in uniform
Lived all their lives in playgrounds
Spent the years inventing games
That don't let me in. Games
That are rough, that swallow you up.

And the railings.
All around, the railings.
Are they to keep out wolves and monsters?
Things that carry off and eat children?
Things you don't take sweets from?
Perhaps they're to stop us getting out
Running away from the lessins. Lessin.
What does a lessin look like?
Sounds small and slimy.
They keep them in the glassrooms.
Whole rooms made out of glass. Imagine.

I wish I could remember my name
Mummy said it would come in useful
Like wellies. When there's puddles.
Yellow wellies. I wish she was here.
I think my name is sewn on somewhere
Perhaps the teacher will read it for me.
Tea-cher. The one who makes the tea.

Roger McGough (1937 –)

From: http://www.poemhunter.com/poem/first-day-at-school/

Understanding Poetry Circle a letter to answer questions 1 to 8.

1. The narrator feels the school is a *million-billion-willion miles from home.*
   The narrator used such a description of the distance because he
   - A   doesn't understand real distances
   - B   is being cheeky and showing off
   - C   is exaggerating to explain his feeling of isolation
   - D   wants his parents to feel sorry for him

2. What does the narrator thinks the teacher does?
   - A   teaches the class
   - B   makes the tea
   - C   keeps small, slimy things
   - D   lives in a glassroom

3. How did the narrator feel about his first day at school?
   - A   he was prepared
   - B   he was excited
   - C   he was startled
   - D   he was overwhelmed

4. The narrator wishes someone could
   - A   read his name tag
   - B   remove all the railings
   - C   tell the teacher his name
   - D   protect him from wolves

5. The railings at the school worries the narrator because
   - A   he thinks wild animals are caged in classrooms
   - B   he doesn't know what they are really for
   - C   they stop children from going to 'lessins'
   - D   they stop monsters from handing out sweets

6. The narrator finds it odd that
   - A   no one steps in puddles
   - B   sweets are handed out to children
   - C   everyone knows what to do
   - D   some people want him to join their game

7. The narrator thinks he should have *wellies. Wellies* are
   - A   wet weather boots
   - B   part of the school uniform
   - C   a name tag
   - D   protection from monsters

8. Who does the narrator miss most of all on his first day at school?
   - A   his teacher
   - B   someone to play with
   - C   someone with sweets
   - D   his mother

Understanding Year 4 Comprehension
A. Horsfield © Five Senses Education © W. Marlin

Doodle Bug

Parent / guardian information

Doodle Bug is an action-shooting sketched hero who fights off <u>waves</u> of aliens, robots and ogres. There's relentless shooting (Doodle, never has to reload!) but no blood!
The game is more of a boy's classroom daydream. There are several in-app purchase opportunities, but they are not necessary to enjoy the game. Coin credits can be earned through good gameplay.

Educational level
Don't buy it for learning. *Doodle Bug* has no educational value. It's for fun!

What's it about?
As Doodle, the hand-drawn hero, players attempt to rescue a kidnapped maiden by fighting their way through droves of enemies, most of which are scribble creatures, the kind a student might draw when bored. Slain enemies drop extra-life hearts, shields, coins, and other items (which can be upgraded using in-game credits). When players die, they can reverse time and play with the assistance of their ghost.

What's its value?
Doodle Bug is a fast game that takes a common storyline and improves it with creative extras. From the choice of weapons or one of your ghosts, the game can be challenging,but not annoying - and never impossible.

The animations are delightful and while the violence is too much for very young players, it's satisfactory for older kids. It is blood-free and cartoonish. The awkward layout of some buttons is a minor fault. Players will be occupied having fun shooting their way to the distressed maiden.

Suitable for 10 years old
Free
Quality: 4 stars
Learning: 1 star

Understanding Reports Circle a letter or write an answer for questions 1 to 8.

1. The purpose of this review is to
    A   convince teachers to use the game in the classroom
    B   persuade parents to buy the game as a fun game
    C   teach children how to use guns
    D   warn users of the dangers of the game

2. What does Doodle Bug look like?
    A   a super hero   B   a cowboy
    C   a scribbled person   D   a monster

3. How does the reviewer rate the game
    A   very good   B   not bad
    C   okay   D   boring

4. Many monsters and ogres get shot. What is unusual about this?
    A   they monsters and ogres return as ghosts
    B   there is no blood from the wounds
    C   the bullets pass straight through their bodies
    D   those hit by bullets are not hurt

5. The word *waves* as used in paragraph 1 refers
    A   moving hands about to attract attention
    B   ridges of water formed in oceans
    C   rocking back and forth on the one spot
    D   anything that returns time and time again

6. What does the reviewer think the game story is most like?
    A   a violent TV cartoon   B   an action-hero comic
    C   a boy's classroom daydream   D   an ancient myth or legend

7. This review is most likely for
    A   parents   B   teachers   C   game players   D   illustrators

8. In your own words briefly describe what a *doodle* is.

Write your answer on the line. It is a _____

Need to try another report? Check the contents page.

Lit Tip 39 – Improve your literacy skills   **Using the ellipsis correctly**

An ellipsis is a set of dots (…) that indicate that something is left out or not said.

Note: ellipsis (singular) – ellipses (more than one). Ellipses have three dots, no more!

They can be used to

*   show a pause: "I'm wondering … " said Paul quietly.

*   show hesitation: I wasn't really … I mean … you see …

*   indicate words omitted on purpose but the intended meaning is clear.

    Dad said, "You didn't eat the cabbage, so … (Dad is making a bit of a threat.)

Note: Commas or full stops do not follow an ellipsis.

Ellipses are often overused in some students' writing. This is not a good technique.

Understanding Year 4 Comprehension
A. Horsfield © Five Senses Education © W. Marlin

Black Beauty extract

(Black Beauty by Anna Sewell is about a horse that must be 'broken in', that is, trained to accept a rider. Black Beauty recounts her experience. A bit and bridle have been put in place. Now read on.)

Next came the saddle, but that was not half so bad. My master, Squire Gordon, put it on my back very gently, while old Daniel held my head. Then he made the girths fast under my body, patting and talking to me all the time. I was then given some oats before being led about.

My master did this every day until I began to look for the oats and the saddle. Finally, one morning, my master got on my back and rode me round the meadow on the soft grass. It certainly did feel queer, but I must say I felt rather proud to carry my master. He continued to ride me a little every day and I soon became accustomed to it.

The next unpleasant business was putting on the iron shoes. That too was very hard at first. My master went with me to the blacksmith's forge, to see that I was not hurt or frightened.

The blacksmith took my feet in his hand, one after the other, and cut away some of the hoof. It did not hurt at all, so I stood still on three legs until he had done them all.

Then the blacksmith took a piece of iron the shape of my foot, and clapped it on, and drove some nails through the shoe right into my hoof, so that the shoe was firmly fixed in place. My feet felt very stiff and heavy, but in time I got used to it.

adapted from the book by Anna Sewell (1820 – 1878)

Understanding Narratives   Circle a letter to answer questions 1 to 8.

1. Who is the narrator of the text?
    A   Squire Gordon   B   old Daniel
    C   Anna Sewell   D   Black Beauty

2. Which word best describes Black Beauty?
    A   placid   B   stubborn   C   impulsive   D   timid

3. What was the last thing Black Beauty had to get used to?
    A   saddle   B   bit and bridle
    C   horseshoes   D   girths

4. When a horse is 'broken in' it has
    A   been trained to accept a rider   B   broken into the stable
    C   been hurt in a fall   D   been beaten until it obeys commands

5. How did Black Beauty respond to having her first horseshoes?
    She found it
    A   an uncomfortable experience   B   a spiteful experience
    C   an expected experience   D   a painful experience

6. To get Black Beauty to accept a saddle Squire Gordon
    A   patted her and talked to her all the time
    B   took one hoof in his hand at the time
    C   got old Daniel to hold her head
    D   rewarded her with a feed of oats before each ride

7. The text *Black Beauty* is written in
    A   past tense   B   present tense   C   future tense

8. If this text had a title, a suitable title would be
    A   Early morning ride
    B   A new experience
    C   Saddle and oats
    D   Meeting the blacksmith

Lit Tip 40 – Improve your literacy skills   Better story endings

One of the more difficult things to do when writing a story is to have a good ending.

The ending must solve the problem the character faces in a way that leaves the reader feeling satisfied. That's why these endings are not really acceptable:

*   I woke up and it was all a dream (or nightmare)
*   I said some magic words and I was safe
*   A superhero suddenly saved me from a terrifying disaster
*   They lived happily ever after!

These suggest to the reader you had no idea how to end your story.

And some bad beginnings:

Once upon a time   AND   The night was dark and stormy

Understanding Year 4 Comprehension
A. Horsfield © Five Senses Education © W. Marlin

1. Who is the narrator of the text?
    A. Squire Gordon   B. old Daniel
    C. Anna Sewell   D. Black Beauty

2. Which word best describes Black Beauty?
    A. placid   B. stubborn   C. impulsive   D. timid

3. What was the last thing Black Beauty had to get used to?
    A. saddle   B. bit and bridle
    C. horseshoes   D. girths

4. When a horse is 'broken in' it has
    A. been trained to accept a rider   B. broken into the stable
    C. been hurt in a fall   D. been beaten until it obeys commands

5. How did Black Beauty respond to having her first horseshoes?
    She found it
    A. an uncomfortable experience   B. a spiteful experience
    C. an expected experience   D. a painful experience

6. To get Black Beauty to accept a saddle, Squire Gordon
    A. patted her and talked to her all the time
    B. took one hoof in his hand at the time
    C. got old Daniel to hold her head
    D. rewarded her with a feed of oats before each ride

7. The text Black Beauty is written in
    A. past tense   B. present tense   C. future tense

8. If this text had a title a suitable title would be
    A. Early morning ride
    B. A new experience
    C. Saddle and oats
    D. Meeting the blacksmith

Lit Tip 40 – improve your literacy skills   Better story endings

One of the more difficult things to do when writing a story is to have a good ending.

The ending must solve the problem the character faces in a way that leaves the reader
feeling satisfied. That's why these endings are not easily acceptable:

- I woke up and it was all a dream (or nightmare).
- I said some magic words and I was safe.
- A sugar herb suddenly saved me from a terrifying disaster.
- They lived happily ever after.

These suggest to the reader you had no idea how to end your story.

And some bad beginnings:

- Once upon a time. AND The night was dark and stormy.

82

SOLUTIONS

Understanding Year 4 Comprehension
A. Horsfield © Five Senses Education © W. Marlin

Answers

Year 4 Comprehension Questions

No.   Title   Answers

1. The Carousel: 1. B   2. D   3. C   4. B   5. B   6. C   7. an old grandstand   8. A

2. Animal Houses: 1. B   2. D   3. A   4. C   5. FALSE   6. D   7. D kennel   8. A

3. Green Tea: 1. B   2. D   3. A   4. D   5. B   6. C   7. black tea OR coffee   8. D

4. Ice cream: 1. C   2. C   3. D   4. A   5. B   6. A   7. dribbles   8. D

5. Fiji Postcard:1. B   2. C   3. A   4. C   5. D   6. C   7. A   8. (2, 1, 4, 3)

6. Battery Drain: 1. C   2. A   3. B   4. D   5. A   6. C   7. D   8. B

7. Gillang Bay: 1. A   2. A   3. D   4. B   5. C   6. chugged   7. B   8. false

8. Insects: 1. C   2. A   3. D   4. D   5. A   6. D   7. three (3)   8. C

9. Library Rules: 1. D   2. B   3. A   4. D   5. A   6. B   7. D   8. (1, 4, 3, 2)

10. Sheep Sheep:1. D   2. C   3. A   4. B   5. C   6. D   7. A   8. D

11. Comics and Cartoons: 1. A   2. (2)   3. C   4. B   5. D   6. C   7. B   8. B

12. Mr Tom Narrow: 1. B   2. A   3. D   4. A   5. C   6. B   7. C   8. True

13. What is an Adverb? 1. C   2. A   3. D   4. C   5. Answers vary: (e.g. loudly)   6. B   7. A   8. A

14. Sending Parcels: 1. B   2. B   3. Express   4. A   5. D   6. C   7. A   8. C

15. Read a Real Book!: 1. B   2. A   3. bookworm   4. D   5. A   6. C   7. C   8. A

16. Lost Time: 1. C   2. A   3. B   4. B   5. D   6. C   7. D   8. A

17. Sandcastles and Sand Sculptures: 1. B   2. D   3. B   4. C   5. A   6. C   7. (2, 1, 4, 3)   8. A

18. Teddy Bears' Picnic: 1. A   2. B   3. C   4. C   5. Because   6. B   7. C   8. A

19. The Bermuda Triangle: 1. D   2. A   3. B   4. C   5. D   6. (1, 4, 3, 2)   7. C   8. B

20. *Where's Wally?* hits Major Milestone: 1. A   2. C   3. B   4. D   5. B   6. C   7. Waldo   8. A

Continued on the next page...

No.	Title				Answers				

21. Madeleine Says: 1. B 2. A 3. D 4. A 5. C 6. B 7. A 8. C

22. Nasrudin's Choice: 1. D 2. A 3. A 4. D 5. (2, 4, 3, 1) 6. C 7. B 8. B

23. Energy In - Energy Out: 1. D 2. A 3. jellybeans 4. D 5. C 6. A 7. C 8. B

24. Meet Bruiser: 1. A 2. B 3. C 4. B 5. D 6. C 7. A 8. D

25. Summer Adventure: 1. C 2. C 3. D 4. A 5. D 6. B 7. A 8. B

26. Letter to the Editor: 1. B 2. C 3. D 4. A 5. C 6. B 7. YES 8. D

27. Headphones: 1. D 2. B 3. C 4. A 5. B 6. C 7. A 8. D

28. Parts of a Knife: 1. B 2. A 3. C 4. D 5. A 6. C 7. B 8. C

29. Home page: Norseman: 1. B 2. D 3. A 4. C 5. C 6. B 7. (145 or 145.6) 8. D

30. Be Glad Your Nose is on Your Face: 1. A 2. C 3. D 4. B 5. toes 6. B 7. A 8. D

31. The Mary Celeste Mystery: 1. B 2. C 3. D 4. D 5. (1, 4, 2, 3) 6. C 7. A 8. C

32. Strange Meeting: 1. D 2. A 3. A 4. B 5. C 6. B 7. D 8. A

33. How Fog Lights Work: 1. C 2. TRUE 3. A 4. B 5. D 6. B 7. Drawbacks 8. A

34. Gillang Bay at Night: 1. D 2. lanterns OR torches 3. C 4. D 5. B 6. C 7. A 8. B

35. Potato Prints: 1. B 2. C 3. B 4. A 5. D 6. (3, 1, 2, 4) 7. D 8. C

36. Puppy Class Flier: 1. B 2. D 3. TRUE 4. A 5. B 6. C 7. A 8. D

37. Sir Donald Bradman: 1. A 2. B 3. TRUE 4. B 5. D 6. (2, 4, 3, 1) 7. C 8. B

38. First Day at School: 1. C 2. B 3. D 4. A 5. B 6. C 7. A 8. D

39. Game Review: 1. B 2. C 3. A 4. B 5. D 6. C 7. A 8. (Suggestion) scribble drawing

40. Black Beauty: 1. D 2. A 3. C 4. A 5. A 6. D 7. A 8. B

Understanding Year 4 Comprehension
A. Horsfield © Five Senses Education © W. Marlin

Year 4 Answers

Lit Tip Exercises

No. Text title	Topic	Answers
1. The Carousel:	Direct / Indirect speech	Examples 1 and 3
2. Animal Houses:	Rhyme	bead, home, brother, fur
3. Green Tea:	How to use dashes	reason/it, Pete Gray (1978 -)
4. Ice Cream:	Synonyms and antonyms	start/finish, tired/drowsy, cold/hot
5. Fiji Postcard:	Compound words	highway, bookmark, television
6. Battery Drain:	Using initials	PIN, UNSW, NAPLAN
7. Gillang Bay:	Similes	tree, chimney, dinner plate
8. Insects:	Full stops with titles	3 (Hon.) 6 (Dep.), Sen., Prof.
9. Library Rules:	The prefix *dis*	1 dishonest, 2 disable(d) 3 disbelieve, 4 dislike
10. Sheep Sheep	Contractions	he is, you are. i, ha, a, i, o, o, wi
11. Cartoons	Apostrophe of possession	1 's for all answers (e.g. man's watch) 2 (the) claw of the tiger
12. Mr Tom Narrow:	Stanza, verse or chorus	four (4), NO
13. What is an Adverb?	Tense	present, past, future
14. Sending Parcels:	Regular verbs	jumped, tossed, tried, skipped, copied, traced
15. Read a Real Book!	Irregular verbs	ate, spoke, saw, blew, bought said, forgotten
16. Lost Time	Proper nouns	Einstein, Tasmania, Bill
17. Sandcastles	Question marks	Oral responses
18. Teddy Bears' Picnic	Person	Second, Third, First, Third
19. Bermuda Triangle	Author or narrator?	Answers will vary.
20. Where's Wally	Deity capitals	2 (Word of God), 4 (Christians)

Continued on the next page...

No. Text title	Topic	Answers
21. Madeleine Says	Redundant words	frozen, down, armed, lost
22. Nasrudin's choice	Affixes	ful, pre, es, s, ing, ly, re, able, un-ed
23. Energy in - Energy out	Interjections	Examples only: Yuk!, Phew!, Ahh!, No!, So!, Thanks!
24. Meet Bruiser	Alliteration	1 w 2 ch 3 sl face (example)
25. Summer adventure	Comparing adjectives	sadder, saddest, tall<u>er</u> (example)
26. Letter to Editor	Rhetorical questions	Why do I ask this question?
27. Headphones	Proper adjectives	French, Canadian, Russian, Greek Mexican, Turk
28. Parts of a Knife	Puns	No written responses.
29. Home page: Norseman	Opposites using prefixes	improper, unable, unfed, untrue unknown, impatient, immature, unread
30. Your Nose Poem	Repetition	rock (rock after rock)
31. Mary Celeste	Homonyms	1 noun, verb 2 verb, noun
32. Strange Meeting	Acronyms or initials	NASA, NAPLAN, TEN (channel), radar
33. How Fog Lights Work	Punctuation in speech	Dad called, "Can you see the bin?"
34. Gillang Bay at Night	Idiom	'in big trouble' or 'in a mess'
35. Potato Prints	Better words than *said*	Suggestions: agreed, hissed, snapped begged, snarled, whispered
36. Puppy Training ad	Dual ownership	Dad and Mum's invitation was lost.
37. Sir Donald Bradman	Writing the date	Answers will vary.
38. First day at School	Using commas	Meg, Ken, Raj and Toni were lost!
39. Game Review	Ellipsis	No responses required.
40. Black Beauty	Bad story endings	No response required.

Understanding Year 4 Comprehension
A. Horsfield © Five Senses Education © W. Marlin

Notes